MATHEMATICAL
M O D E L I N G

No. 1

Edited by
Samuel Goldberg, Oberlin College
William F. Lucas, Cornell University
Henry O. Pollak, Bell Laboratories
Maynard Thompson, University of Indiana

BIRKHÄUSER

Probability in Social Science

Seven Expository Units Illustrating the Use of
Probability Methods and Models, with Exercises, and Bibliographies to
Guide Further Reading in the Social Science and
Mathematics Literatures

by
Samuel Goldberg

Birkhäuser
Boston • Basel • Stuttgart

Samuel Goldberg
Department of Mathematics
Oberlin College
Oberlin, Ohio 44074, USA

This book was set in type by John Knuth on the TEX system, Stanford, which was created by his father, Donald E. Knuth.

Library of Congress Cataloging in Publication Data
Goldberg, Samuel I.
  Probability in social science.

  (Mathematical modelling ; 1)
  1. Social sciences--Statistical methods.
2. Social sciences--Mathematical models.
3. Probabilities. I. Title. II. Series:
Mathematical modelling (Cambridge, Mass.) ; 1.
HA29.G638   300'.1'5192   82-4470
ISBN 3-7643-3089-9   AACR2

CIP–Kurztitelaufnahme der Deutschen Bibliothek

Goldberg, Samuel;
Probability in social science : 7 expository
units illustrating the use of probability methods
and models, with exercises, and bibliogr. to
guide further reading in the social science and
math. literatures / Samuel Goldberg. - Boston ;
Basel ; Stuttgart : Birkhäuser, 1982.
  (Mathematical modelling ; No. 1) .
  ISBN 3-7646-3089-9

NE: GT

© Birkhäuser Boston, Inc., 1983

ISBN 3-7643-3089-9 (hardcover); 3-7643-3128-3 (paperback)

Printed in USA

iv

Editors' Preface

Birkhäuser Boston, Inc., will publish a series of carefully selected mono-graphs in the area of mathematical modeling to present serious applications of mathematics for both the undergraduate and the professional audience.

Some of the monographs to be selected and published will appeal more to the professional mathematician and user of mathematics, serving to familiarize the user with new models and new methods. Some, like the present monograph, will stress the educational aspect and will appeal more to a student audience, either as a textbook or as additional reading.

We feel that this first volume in the series may in itself serve as a model for our program. Samuel Goldberg attaches a high priority to teaching stu-dents the art of modeling, that is, to use his words, the art of constructing useful mathematical models of real-world phenomena. We concur. It is our strong conviction as editors that the connection between the actual problems and their mathematical models must be factually plausible, if not actually real.

As this first volume in the new series goes to press, we invite its readers to share with us both their criticisms and their constructive suggestions.

The Editors

Preface

This book illustrates the use of probability ideas and techniques in the social sciences. Recent curriculum reports* have emphasized the importance of applications for the undergraduate mathematics curriculum. The present work includes seven expository articles intended to acquaint readers with a variety of widely used probabilistic models within social science and to bring out some basic features of mathematical modeling.

I do not imply in offering this volume that social science models are more ideal for illustrating applications of probability than other subjects. A similar set of articles using examples from biology and medicine, from the physical sciences and engineering, from business and law, could (and should) also be prepared. What is important is less the subject matter of the applications than the spur to teachers and students to spend more time in their probability courses (and in other mathematics courses, too) discussing applications. Developing in their students the art of modeling, that is, of constructing a useful mathematical model of some real-world phenomenon, should be a higher priority than it now is for departments of mathematics. Although a very difficult task for teachers, we must not shy away on that account. Of course, reading about applications and modeling is quite different from the activity of mathematical modeling itself. Bringing illustrative examples of the sort presented in this volume into the classroom is one way of easing into the more challenging task.

Applications in demography, linguistics, management science, political science, psychology, and sociology are included in our seven chapters. Although the boundary lines between different social sciences are fuzzy and economists are likely to be interested in many of these applications, no unit on economics itself is included. There is already a vast literature on mathematical economics, and probabilistic models still appear to be less important than deterministic optimization techniques in economic theory.**

---

*The Role of Applications in the Undergraduate Mathematics Curriculum, National Research Council, Washington, D.C., 1979; Recommendations for a General Mathematical Science Program, Committee on the Undergraduate Program in Mathematics, The Mathematical Association of America, Washington, D.C., 1981.

**There is however a considerable literature on probabilistic economics, since uncertainty plays a crucial role in economic behavior. See, for example, Lippman, S. A. and J. J. McCall, "The Economics of Uncertainty: Selected Topics and Probabilistic Methods," pp.211–284 in Arrow, K. J. and M. D. Intriligator (Eds.), Handbook of Mathematical Economics, vol. 1, Amsterdam: North Holland, 1981. These authors' bibliography will lead the interested reader to many other books and journal articles on probability models in economics.

As the accompanying bibliographies indicate, particular topics reviewed here are of relatively current interest. Of the 208 citations to articles and books, 10% are dated prior to 1960, 34% in the 1960s, 46% in the 1970s, and 10% in the 1980s. Nevertheless, no claim is being made that important contributions to social science are represented here. I am not qualified to make that judgment, which should be left to social scientists themselves. I can attest to two important facts which led to the selection of these particular topics: 1) they illustrate probability theory as it is actually used by social scientists, and 2) they supply a context for discussing applications of probability theory that interest and intrigue many students. As any teacher of mathematics knows very well, getting the attention and interest of one's students is more than half the battle.

This book can be used in a number of different ways. As a supplement to a standard post-calculus probability course, it would allow students to see how the ideas and techniques they are learning are used in the social sciences. It was with this use in mind that the book was kept short and therefore relatively inexpensive. Exercises appear at the end of each chapter, along with bibliographic notes to guide further reading in the social science and mathematics literatures. Each chapter stands on its own and can be read without regard to the others. The little overlap this produces seems to me to be a price worth paying for the added flexibility obtained in making course assignments.

In almost every unit, students will see more than just familiar material from a probability course. Their experience with differential and integral calculus, power series expansions, matrix algebra, and differential equations will be broadened and made more meaningful. In Chapter 3, the elements of dynamic programming and the discounting of cash flows are introduced. In Chapters 2 and 5, there is an introduction to stochastic processes, with expositions of birth-death and Yule processes. Important connections between deterministic and stochastic models are pointed out. Chapter 5 also contains an explanation of the important statistical idea of maximum likelihood estimation. The elements of the theory of finite Markov chains are introduced (without proofs) in Chapter 6. In short, there is much of value here beyond merely a review of material from a first course in probability.

A separate note on prerequisites is included to indicate what parts of a probability course are required to read each chapter in this book. As is noted there, two chapters and half of a third depend only on discrete probabilities and do not require a calculus background.

Teachers planning a course on applications of mathematics or seeking resource or reference material for seminars and independent reading courses on applications or modeling may also find the book of some interest. I would be disappointed if social scientists did not also find material here of value to themselves and their students.

Comments from readers are always welcome.

Brookline, Massachusetts   Samuel Goldberg
March 23, 1982

Acknowledgements

The chapters in this book are significantly modified versions of units initially written by me as editor of a joint project of the Mathematical Social Science Board and the Committee on the Undergraduate Program in Mathematics of the Mathematical Association of America. This project, sponsored by the National Science Foundation, resulted in the sourcebook *Some Illustrative Examples of the Use of Undergraduate Mathematics in the Social Sciences*, distributed by the MAA in 1977. Seven of the fifteen units in the sourcebook have been modified, some only a little, others more drastically, for this volume. Bibliographies have been updated and expanded. Exercises, absent in the sourcebook, have been added to each chapter.

Members of the Editorial Board for the MSSB-MAA project were John Chipman, R. Duncan Luce, James G. March, Henry O. Pollak, and Edward L. Spitznagel, Jr. Also receiving a draft of the fifteen units of the sourcebook and participating in its review were Donald W. Bushaw and George Pedrick, then Chairman and Executive Director, respectively, of CUPM. To assist in generating examples for the project, the MSSB organized three panels of social scientists. These were chaired by Michael Intriligator (Economics), Duncan Luce (Psychology), and Roy D'Andrade (Other Social Sciences). Glottochronology, the topic of Chapter 5, was brought to my attention by Robert Wall in notes prepared for the project. The stochastic model in Chapter 7 was outlined in notes on memory search mechanisms submitted to the Psychology Panel by Jean-Claude Falmagne and Geoffrey Iverson. I am very grateful to all of these colleagues for their help with the sourcebook.

A sabbatical leave from Oberlin College gave me the time to prepare this volume. Long live sabbaticals! The work was done while I was a visitor at Harvard University's School of Public Health. I am indebted to Howard S. Frazier, Director of the Center for the Analysis of Health Practices, and Marvin Zelen, Chairman of the Department of Biostatistics, for their hospitality. A grant from the Alfred P. Sloan Foundation made it possible to extend my leave over the full academic year, and I am grateful to the Officers of the Foundation for their support.

My wife, Marcia, typed the entire manuscript with her customary superb style. She was her usual tolerant self in spite of the pressure to meet deadlines. To her go very special thanks.

Note to the Reader about Prerequisites

It is assumed that readers will be familiar with the techniques of differential and integral calculus for functions of one variable, including infinite series and Maclaurin power series expansions. Chapter 6 requires an acquaintance with matrix algebra. However, Chapters 1 and 4 and the first half of Chapter 3 depend only on discrete probability and can be read without a calculus background.

The chart below indicates which topics in a standard probability course are prerequisite for chapters in this book. The location of a chapter number corresponds to the point in the syllabus when an adequate background for understanding the content of that chapter would normally have been acquired.

Probability Topics	*Chapter*
Basic rules of probability; finite sample spaces; counting techniques (permutations, combinations, binomial coefficients).	1
Conditional probability; independent events; multiplication rule for probability of joint occurrence of events.	3 (Problem 1)
Discrete random variables; probability mass function; distribution function; Bernoulli trials and binomial distribution; mean and variance; geometric, Poisson distributions; $E(X + Y) = E(X) + E(Y)$.	2*, 4, 5*
Continuous random variables; probability density function; distribution function; uniform, exponential, normal, and gamma distributions; mean and variance; independent random variables.	3 (Problem 2), 6**
Further topics: moment generating functions; sums of random variables; convolution integral.	7

---

*These chapters contain detailed expositions of birth-death (Chapter 2) and Yule pure death (Chapter 5) stochastic processes. No prior knowledge of stochastic processes is assumed.

**Some basic definitions and results for finite Markov chains, needed in this chapter, are presented without proofs.

Table of Contents

Chapter 1
A Power Index for Individuals and Coalitions

1. Introduction

"Power is a major explanatory concept in the study of social choice. It is used in studies of relations among nations, of community decision making, of business behavior, and of small-group discussion. Partly because it conveys simultaneously overtones of the cynicism of *Realpolitik*, the glories of classical mechanics, the realism of elite sociology, and the comforts of anthropocentric theology, *power* provides a prime focus for disputation and exhortation in several social sciences." (March [26, p.39].) A general exposition of the notion of power and of attempts to study and explain politics by analyzing power relationships is given by Dahl [11].

Our aim in this unit is much more modest. It is to define and discuss some applications of the so-called Shapley-Shubik power index, a numerical measure of the power of individuals and of coalitions of individuals in decision-making voting bodies. This measure of power originates in concepts of game theory. Although a development of these general concepts would take us too far afield, we are able to illustrate the basic ideas by reference to a special three-person game. This will lead to the definition of the power index of a member or group of members of a voting body. Some illustrative examples will show how the index is computed using the familiar counting techniques involving permutations and combinations. References to further applications as well as to discussions of other indices of power, especially the Banzhaf index, conclude the unit.

2. Coalitions and Characteristic Function of a Game

The game we shall consider is a slight modification of the "Left-Right" game in Rapoport [35]. There are three players. Player 1 moves first and says "Yes" (Y) or "No" (N). Player 2, having heard player 1's choice, also chooses Y or N. Finally, player 3, knowing both prior choices, makes his own choice of Y or N. Figure 1 indicates the eight possible sequences of choices and the corresponding payoffs accruing to player 1, 2, and 3 respectively. Thus, if each player chooses Y then player 1 receives 1 unit and each of the other players receives 4 units. But if player 1's choice of Y is followed by a Y and then an N, the payoff to player 1 is 4 units, player 2 gives up 1 unit (since the payoff is negative), and player 3 receives 6 units.

1

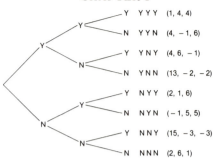

Figure 1. Yes-No Game. Each player chooses Y or N, starting with player 1. Player 2 knows player 1's choice; player 3 knows choices of both players 1 and 2. Payoffs to players are given in parentheses next to each possible sequence of choices.

Note that the sum of the three payoffs is 9 for every sequence of choices. The game is therefore called *constant-sum*. (No particular significance attaches to the value of the constant. We could, for example, make this game zero-sum by subtracting three from each payoff.)

Let us review player 1's thoughts as he contemplates his choice. *Each player is assumed to play selfishly so as to get the largest possible payoff for himself.* If player 1 chooses Y, player 2 must follow with Y or N. If the former, then player 3 will follow with N and player 2 will end up with -1 unit. If, on the other hand, player 2 follows with N, then player 3 will choose Y and player 2 ends up with 6 units. Clearly, player 2's self-interest leads him to choose N if player 1 chooses Y, resulting in the sequence YNY and a payoff to player 1 of 4 units. If player 1 chooses N a similar analysis shows that player 2 will follow with N and player 3 with N, thus getting player 1 a payoff of 2 units. As between Y and N, therefore, player 1 chooses Y since it gives him a larger payoff. And we have seen that the outcome of the game is then the sequence YNY.

Now suppose we allow players to act *together* in order to obtain the largest *joint* payoff they can. If player 1 chooses Y, players 2 and 3 can, by agreeing to cooperate, bring the game to the outcome YYY which gives them a joint payoff of 8 units and gives a 1 unit payoff to player 1. But if player 1 chooses N, then players 2 and 3, by cooperating, will produce the outcome NYN which gives them a joint payoff of 10 units and gives a -1 unit payoff to player 1. Player 1, in the face of this organized opposition, will therefore choose Y and receive 1 unit, leading as we have seen to a joint payoff of 8 units to the cooperating pair of players 2 and 3. We say that the *value* of the game to the coalition $\{2,3\}$ is 8 and the value to the coalition $\{1\}$ made up of player 1 himself is 1 unit. In symbols

$$v(\{1\}) = 1, \qquad v(\{2,3\}) = 8. \tag{1}$$

Now consider what player 2's best choice is when he faces the coalition $\{1,3\}$. If player 1 chooses Y, player 2 will also choose Y (and lose 1 unit since player 3 will choose N) rather than choose N (and lose 2 units since player 3 will again choose N). Thus if player 1 chooses Y, player 2 will follow with Y and player 3 with N giving the coalition $\{1,3\}$ the joint payoff of 10 units. On the other hand, if player 1 starts with N, player 2 will be better off choosing Y (gaining 1 unit when player 3 follows with Y rather than losing 3 units by choosing N which player 3 follows with Y). In this case the coalition $\{1,3\}$ will get only 8 units. Hence the coalition begins the game with the agreement that player 1 will choose Y. The values are thus found to be

$$v(\{2\}) = -1, \qquad v(\{1,3\}) = 10. \tag{2}$$

Similar reasoning shows that if players 1 and 2 form a coalition, then their best choices are Y and N (since then their joint payoff is at least 10) and player 3 follows with Y and loses 1 unit. Hence

$$v(\{3\}) = -1, \qquad v(\{1,2\}) = 10. \tag{3}$$

If all three players get together, this so-called *grand coalition* of all players surely is guaranteed a joint payoff of 9 units since the sum of the payoffs is 9 for all possible choices of the players. Since this grand coalition opposes the *null coalition* (denoted by $\emptyset$) it is reasonable to define the value of the game as zero for this coalition containing no players:

$$v(\emptyset) = 0, \qquad v(\{1,2,3\}) = 9. \tag{4}$$

The collection of eight values given in (1)–(4), one value for each of the eight ($= 2^3$) possible subsets of the three players, defines the so-called *characteristic function* of this Yes-No game. In general, for an n-person constant-sum ($= k$) game the characteristic function is a function whose domain is the set of all subsets (coalitions) of the universal set (grand coalition)

$$I_n = \{1, 2, \ldots, n\},$$

and which assigns a real-number value $v(A)$ to each of these 2^n subsets. These values satisfy the following conditions*:

(i) $v(\emptyset) = 0$
(ii) $v(I_n) = k$
(iii) $v(\overline{A}) = k - v(A)$ $\qquad\qquad\qquad$ (5)
(iv) $v(A \cup B) \geq v(A) + v(B), \qquad$ if $A \cap B = \emptyset$.

---

*We use the usual symbolism of set theory. $\overline{A}$ denotes the *complement* of A with respect to the universal set I_n, $A \cup B$ is the *union* and $A \cap B$ the *intersection* of the two coalitions A and B. The condition $A \cap B = \emptyset$ simply means that no player belongs to both A and B.

Using the values (1)–(4) it is easy to verify that these conditions are satisfied for the Yes-No game summarized in Figure 1. In general, the value $v(A)$ is the value of the two-person game in which the coalition A plays as a single player with the complementary countercoalition $\overline{A}$ as the opposing player. For further details, consult Luce and Raiffa [23] or Owen [31]. These conditions need not be satisfied for *non*-constant-sum games (see Exercise 1), but constant-sum games suffice for óur present purpose of defining a power index for each player in a game and so we can assume henceforth that conditions (i)–(iv) are satisfied.

3. Shapley Value to a Player

The characteristic function of an n-person game gives a value for *each coalition* A of I_n but it does not give us a breakdown that allows assigning some part of $v(A)$ to *each individual player* making up coalition A. This task was solved by Shapley [43] in 1953 and we turn now to the determination of the so-called *Shapley value* for each player in the game.

It will be helpful to illustrate the basic ideas involved by reference to the Yes-No game whose characteristic function we have already computed and which we summarize here for convenience:

$$
\begin{aligned}
&v(\emptyset) = 0 \\
&v(\{1\}) = 1, \qquad v(\{2\}) = v(\{3\}) = -1 \\
&v(\{1,2\}) = v(\{1,3\}) = 10, \qquad v(\{2,3\}) = 8 \\
&v(\{1,2,3\}) = 9.
\end{aligned}
\tag{6}
$$

Think of building up the grand coalition by a sequence of additions of one player at a time, starting from the empty coalition $\emptyset$. There are six ($= 3!$) possible orderings to consider:

$$
\begin{aligned}
&\emptyset \to \{1\} \to \{1,2\} \to \{1,2,3\} \\
&\emptyset \to \{1\} \to \{1,3\} \to \{1,3,2\} \\
&\emptyset \to \{2\} \to \{2,1\} \to \{2,1,3\} \\
&\emptyset \to \{2\} \to \{2,3\} \to \{2,3,1\} \\
&\emptyset \to \{3\} \to \{3,1\} \to \{3,1,2\} \\
&\emptyset \to \{3\} \to \{3,2\} \to \{3,2,1\}
\end{aligned}
\tag{7}
$$

In any such sequence, if A is a coalition not containing player i and one adds i to form the larger coalition $A \cup \{i\}$, then the value has changed from $v(A)$ to $v(A \cup \{i\})$. *The incremental value $v(A \cup \{i\}) - v(A)$ is credited to player i.* As Riker and Ordeshook [39, p.158] characterize this convention:

> The last member, sequentially and chronologically, gets the increment, as might happen if each person were able to insist on receiving his marginal contribution to the value of the coalition. Where players are able to withhold membership—and hence contributions—this is a common rule.

To illustrate, consider the contributions credited to player 2 in the orderings listed in (7). In the first ordering, player 2, when he forms the coalition $\{1,2\}$, is credited with

$$v(\{1,2\}) - v(\{1\}) = 10 - 1 = 9 \text{ units.}$$

In the second ordering, player 2, when he forms the coalition $\{1,3,2\}$, is credited with

$$v(\{1,3,2\}) - v(\{1,3\}) = 9 - 10 = -1 \text{ unit.}$$

And in the remaining four orderings, player 2 can similarly be seen to get $v(\{2\}) - v(\emptyset) = -1$, $v(\{2\}) - v(\emptyset) = -1$, $v(\{3,1,2\}) - v(\{3,1\}) = -1$, and $v(\{3,2\}) - v(\{3\}) = 9$ units, respectively.

Assuming all six possible orderings are equally likely, the *average or expected incremental value* credited to player 2 is

$$v_2 = \frac{(9) + (-1) + (-1) + (-1) + (-1) + (9)}{6}$$

or $7/3$ units. This is the Shapley value of the Yes-No game to player 2. In a similar way, one can find that the Shapley value to player 1 is $v_1 = 13/3$ and to player 3 is $v_3 = 7/3$ units. Note that these Shapley values have sum equal to 9, the value assigned to the grand coalition $\{1,2,3\}$ by the characteristic function in (6).

From this example we make the straightforward generalization for an n-person game whose characteristic function is known. *Consider all $n!$ possible orderings of the n players. (Each ordering determines exactly one sequence of additions, one player at a time, starting with $\emptyset$ and ending with the grand coalition I_n.) Suppose these orderings are equally likely so each has probability $1/n!$. In each ordering, if player i is the last member of the coalition $A \cup \{i\}$, where A is a coalition not containing i, then player i receives an amount equal to the incremental value $v(A \cup \{i\}) - v(A)$. The expected (or mean) value of these amounts is the Shapley value v_i to player i of the game.**

An explicit formula can be obtained for v_i. For among all $n!$ orderings of the n players, we can count those with player i in the $(k+1)$st position. This means i joins a coalition A_k made up of exactly k players. There are $k!$ ways of ordering these k players (merely permuting the members of A_k) and after player i takes his place, the remaining $(n-k-1)$ players can be ordered in $(n-k-1)!$ ways. Hence there are $k!(n-k-1)!$ permutations (among the total $n!$ permutations) which have player i in the $(k+1)$st position, having just joined coalition A_k. In each of these orders player i

---

*Shapley starts with a set of axioms that the values v_i should satisfy and shows they determine v_i uniquely. We have simply described the end result. See Luce and Raiffa [23] or Owen [31] for the axiomatic development.

receives $v(A_k \cup \{i\}) - v(A_k)$. This incremental value is weighted by the factor

$$p_{n,k} = \frac{k!\,(n-k-1)!}{n!} \tag{8}$$

in computing the mean incremental value received by player i. Hence the Shapley value of the game to player i is given by

$$v_i = \sum_{A_k \subset I_n} p_{n,k}[v(A_k \cup \{i\}) - v(A_k)] \tag{9}$$

where, as indicated, the sum is taken over all coalitions of the n players. (If A_k includes player i then $A_k \cup \{i\} = A_k$ and the corresponding term in brackets reduces to zero. Hence the sum in (9) can be taken over only those coalitions of the n players that do *not* contain player i.)

4.   Shapley-Shubik Power Index

Finally we come to the power index which applies the Shapley value to legislative or decision-making games where the players can be considered as voters. Each player has a certain number of votes and the rules of the body establish what total vote count (majority, two-thirds, etc.) is required to pass a motion. For such a game we assume only *winning coalitions* (i.e., those having enough votes to pass a motion) have positive value, and that all other coalitions, whether losing or blocking, have no value. With appropriate normalization, we can suppose all winning coalitions have value 1 and all non-winning coalitions have value 0.* In this case, the incremental value $v(A_k \cup \{i\}) - v(A_k)$ appearing in the sum in (9) will be 0 if both A_k and $A_k \cup \{i\}$ are winning or if both are non-winning coalitions. We cannot have A_k winning and $A_k \cup \{i\}$ non-winning, so the only remaining possibility is that $A_k \cup \{i\}$ is winning, but A_k is non-winning. In this case the incremental value is 1 and so (9) reduces to

$$v_i = \sum_{A_k \subset I_n} p_{n,k} \tag{10}$$

where the sum is now taken over all coalitions A_k such that A_k is non-winning but $A_k \cup \{i\}$ is winning. In any ordering of all n players in which player i is preceded by such a coalition A_k, we say that player i is the pivot. That is, *player i is the pivot in an ordering if the vote total of the coalition of those players preceding him is insufficient to pass a motion, but the total becomes sufficient and the motion passed as soon as player i joins the coalition.*

The quantity $p_{n,k}$ as defined in (8) is the proportion of all $n!$ orderings of the n players in which player i occupies the $(k + 1)$st position. The sum

---

*The assumption being made here is that the game is *simple*, which means that for every coalition A the value $v(A)$ is either 0 or 1.

in (10) is taken over all those coalitions A_k for which this $(k + 1)$st position makes player i the pivot in the ordering. Thus formula (10) can be rephrased as the following definition in which we adopt the customary terminology and call v_i the Shapley-Shubik *power index* (or power) of player i in the voting body:

Definition. *The Shapley-Shubik power index of a member of a voting body is the number of voting orders (permutations of all the members) in which that member is the pivot, divided by the total number of possible voting orders.*

Finally, we remark that voters may organize into coalitions. Any such coalition will be considered as if it were a single bloc voter having a number of votes equal to the total of the votes of its members. The power index of the coalition can then be computed by the above definition.

This power index is identified with Shapley and Shubik due to a 1954 joint paper [45] in which the authors defined the index and indicated how it could be applied to measuring the distribution of power among members or committees of a legislature. Since then the Shapley-Shubik power index has become well-known and widely applied in political science.

5. Some Illustrative Examples

Example 1. A three-person committee operates under majority rule and each person has one vote. There are $3! = 6$ possible orders in which votes can be cast and the second voter is the pivot in each of these orders. Since each person is the second voter in two of the six orders, the power of each person is $1/3$.

It is easy to see, as in this simple illustration, that if a committee has n voters and the voters have equal votes and are interchangeable, so to speak, then the symmetry of the situation leads to each voter having power $1/n$. That the sum of the powers of all voters equals 1 follows directly from the definition of the power index as a proportion.

Example 2. Consider a two-house legislature in which a majority vote in each house is required to pass a motion. House A has 3 members a_1, a_2, a_3; House B has 7 members b_1, b_2, $\ldots$, b_7. Each legislator has one vote. To compute the power index of each legislator, we first note that the two houses, considered as coalitions, must have the same power. Within each house, symmetry requires each member to have the same power. Hence, each member of House A has power $\frac{1}{3} \times \frac{1}{2} = \frac{1}{6}$ and each member of House B has power $\frac{1}{7} \times \frac{1}{2} = \frac{1}{14}$.

It is interesting to obtain these power indices by direct counting, as required by the Definition. There are $10! = 3{,}628{,}800$ voting orders in all. Legislator b_1 can be pivot only in the following orderings of members:

1) b_1 follows 2 members of House A and 3 members of House B,

2) b_1 follows 3 members of House A and 3 members of House B.

In situation 1), the 2 members of House A can be selected in $\binom{3}{2}$ ways from the available 3 members; the 3 members of House B can be selected in $\binom{6}{3}$ ways from the available 6 members other than b_1. These 5 members can be permuted among the five positions preceding b_1 in 5! ways and the remaining four members can be permuted among the four positions following b_1 in 4! ways. Hence b_1 is pivot in situation 1) in

$$\binom{3}{2}\binom{6}{3} 5!\,4! = 172{,}800$$

orderings of the 10 voters. Similarly, b_1 is pivot in situation 2) in

$$\binom{3}{3}\binom{6}{3} 6!\,3! = 86{,}400$$

orderings. Hence, the power of b_1 is

$$\frac{172{,}800 + 86{,}400}{3{,}628{,}800} = \frac{1}{14}.$$

Clearly, the power index assigned to each member of House B is also $1/14$ and the entire house thus has power $1/2$, in agreement with the values obtained by the simpler indirect argument. As Riker and Ordeshook [39, p.168] comment on a similar example:

> Thus the members of the smaller house have a higher index than the members of the larger house even though the eight [ten in our Example] legislators are in all other ways equal. Perhaps this is why Senators usually have more prestige than Representatives.

This example illustrates the use of counting techniques (permutations and combinations) in computing the power index. Naturally, more realistic examples dealing with actual legislatures will require more complicated analysis and much more computation. But the principle remains the same: count in some systematic way the number of orderings of all voters for which a given member is pivotal.

Example 3. Suppose a nine-member decision-making body uses majority rule and each member has one vote. Each member clearly has power $1/9$. But suppose three members form a coalition. What is the power of this three-member coalition assuming no counter-organization, i.e., assuming the six other members vote as individuals? If we use C to denote the coalition and x to denote an individual member, then all voting orders are of the following types:

$$C\,x\,x\,x\,x\,x\,x$$
$$x\,C\,x\,x\,x\,x\,x$$
$$x\,x\,C\,x\,x\,x\,x$$
$$x\,x\,x\,C\,x\,x\,x$$
$$x\,x\,x\,x\,C\,x\,x$$
$$x\,x\,x\,x\,x\,C\,x$$
$$x\,x\,x\,x\,x\,x\,C$$

Since there are the same number (6! $=$ 720) of voting orders in each of these types, we can compute the power of coalition C by determining the proportion *of these seven* voting orders in which C is the pivot. Remembering that C has three votes, we find that C is pivot when it votes in the third, fourth, or fifth position. Hence the coalition C has power $3/7$. Since the remaining power of $4/7$ is divided equally among the other six members, each has power $2/21$.

Note that the three members of the coalition share power $3/7$ whereas their power as individuals totaled $3/9$. The difference of $6/63 = .095$ is termed the "organizational bonus" by Krislov [20, Table 1].

Krislov and also Schubert [42] have studied the distribution of voting power in a nine-member body because of their interest in the U.S. Supreme Court. Both consider the effectiveness of an organized opposition in reducing the power of protagonist coalitions. For example, we have seen that a three-man coalition has power $3/7$ when the other six members of the body act as individuals. Suppose now that these six individuals organize into two coalitions of size 3. By symmetry, it is clear that each coalition has power $1/3$ and so the original group of three has lost power (from $3/7$ to $1/3$) as a result of this counter-organization.

Intuitively one would expect that counter-organization would always lead to a diminution of power for the original group of three. But as we now show, this is not the case when the six other individuals organize into three coalitions of two members each. Denoting the original coalition by C and the three other coalitions by X, Y, Z, note that all voting orders are of the following types, determined by the position of coalition C: $CXYZ$, $XCYZ$, $XYCZ$, $XYZC$. (There are actually 3! $=$ 6 voting orders of each of these types, obtained by permuting the order of the three coalitions X, Y, and Z.) Since C casts three votes and X, Y, Z two votes each, C is the pivot in the second and third above types. Hence the power of C is now $2/4$, an *increase* from $3/7$ as a result of this less-than-ideal counter-organization.

Both Krislov and Schubert present tables showing how the power of protagonist coalitions of all sizes varies as the remaining members organize in various ways. Table 1 excerpts this information for some possible counter-organizations with a protagonist coalition of size 3. Schubert

Organization of Other Members	Power Indices					
	Protagonist Coalition of Size 3	Other Members				
1, 1, 1, 1, 1, 1	.429	.095 .095 .095 .095 .095 .095				
2, 1, 1, 1, 1	.400	.200 .100 .100 .100 .100				
2, 2, 1, 1	.400	.200 .200 .100 .100				
2, 2, 2	.500	.167 .167 .167				
3, 1, 1, 1	.300	.300 .133 .133 .133				
3, 2, 1	.333	.333 .333 .000				
3, 3	.333	.333 .333				

Table 1. Voting Power of Protagonist Coalition of Size 3 in a Nine-Person Body as Six Remaining Members Organize in Various Ways. From Schubert [42, Table 1].

summarizes the entries in the second column as follows [42, p.474]:

The most interesting case is the problem of organizing to compete against a triple. A single additional triple is maximally effective; *while two triples, or a triple and a pair, provide less effective opposition than the single triple.* Either a single pair, or two pairs, provide (equally) weak opposition; while three pairs is a suicidal defense which results in a *gain in power* for the protagonist triple!

6. Applications and Other Measures of Power

It is a mistake, of course, to think that the complex and multifaceted concept of power as it is variously used by political scientists and others will be captured with all its nuances by such a simplified measure of power as the Shapley-Shubik index. Nevertheless, the index has been very widely applied. General discussions can be found in the books by Brams [6], Riker and Ordeshook [39], and Straffin [48], as well as in Lucas [22]. David, Goldman, and Bain [12] study U. S. party conventions, Mann and Shapley [25] and Merrill [27] the Electoral College, MacRae and Price [24] the Senate, and Riker and Niemi [38] the House of Representatives.

Applications to foreign voting bodies are made by Miller [29] and Straffin [46] (Canada); Owen [32] (Israel); and Riker [36] (France). The United Nations Security Council is considered by Junn [19] and Monjardet [30], as well as by Riker and Ordeshook [39].

In the 1960s the U. S. Supreme Court decided a number of cases that led to a reexamination of many of the then current voting arrangements. Banzhaf [1], Krislov [21], and Riker and Shapley [40] all discuss the relation between voting power and various weighted voting arrangements in light of the 1963 decision in *Grey v. Sanders* that "the conception of political equality ... can mean only one thing—one person, one vote" and the decision the following year in *Reynolds v. Sims* holding that both houses of a bicameral state legislature must be apportioned substantially on a population basis. It was in this connection that Banzhaf in a series of papers [1–4] devised what has since become known as the Banzhaf power index. For each of the 2^n possible coalitions (subsets) of n voters, he asked whether a change in a particular individual's vote (from yea to nay, or vice versa) would alter the outcome. If yes, then that individual's vote is said to be *decisive*. The (absolute) Banzhaf power index of a voter is then defined as the number of that voter's decisive votes divided by 2^n. The greater the number of coalitions in which a voter can affect the outcome, the greater his Banzhaf power index. The *relative* Banzhaf power index is obtained by normalizing so the sum of the indices, taken over all voters, is 1.

The Banzhaf and Shapley-Shubik indices are compared in Brams [6], Dubey and Shapley [13], Owen [31,33], Shapley [44], and Straffin [46]. Fascinating discussions of Justice Harlan's negative comments on the Banzhaf index in his dissenting opinion in *Whitcomb v. Chavis*, a case decided by the Supreme Court in 1970, can be found in Grofman [15] and Merrill [28]. The Banzhaf index was favored in *Ianucci v. Board of Supervisors of Washington County*, decided in 1967 by the New York State Court of Appeals. Imrie [17], Johnson [18], and Lucas [22] discuss the large impact this decision has had on the apportionment of votes in county legislatures.

For modifications of the Banzhaf index, see Merrill [27] and Straffin [46]. A general discussion of some other measures of power is found in Riker [37]. Different measures introduced by Coleman [7,8], Dahl [10], and Rae [34] are related to the Banzhaf index by Dubey and Shapley [13]. These authors also point out the relationship between the Banzhaf indices and certain numerical parameters arising in the study of threshold logic and switching functions in electrical engineering. Finally, it is worth noting the use of the Shapley-Shubik power index by Haefele [16] in environmental studies.

Another approach to the problem of power focuses on the question of who a lobbyist should select to approach in a decision-making body in order to promote a favored proposal. Young [51] uses a "best" lobbying strategy to define power. Ben-Dov and Shilony [5] study the related notion of a member's *importance*, the sensitivity to this member's vote of the proposal's probability of being passed, given the opinions of all the voting members of the body and their susceptibility to influence. "In other words, a person is more important the more a change of his mind matters." There are interesting connections between power indices (Shapley-Shubik or Banzhaf) and this importance measure. These authors present a simple example of a three-person decision-making body in which Mr. 1 has greatest a priori power, Mr. 2 is most important, and Mr. 3, because he is able to be influenced more easily (at lower cost), becomes most important when lobbying is added to the system.

Exercises

1. Compute the characteristic function for the game with the same rules as the Yes-No game of Figure 1 but with payoffs to the three players changed as follows:

$$Y\,Y\,Y \text{ gets payoff } (1,1,1)$$
$$Y\,Y\,N \text{ gets payoff } (0,0,3)$$
$$Y\,N\,Y \text{ gets payoff } (0,3,0)$$
$$Y\,N\,N \text{ gets payoff } (-2,2,2)$$
$$N\,Y\,Y \text{ gets payoff } (3,0,0)$$
$$N\,Y\,N \text{ gets payoff } (2,-2,2)$$
$$N\,N\,Y \text{ gets payoff } (2,2,-2)$$
$$N\,N\,N \text{ gets payoff } (-1,-1,-1).$$

Show that conditions (iii) and (iv) listed in (5) are violated for this game, which is *not* constant-sum. (See Rapoport [35, p.79] where this game, described as a three-person Prisoners' Dilemma game, is analyzed.)

2. A four-person committee requires five votes to pass a measure. Members A and B each cast one vote, C casts two, and D casts three votes. Calculate the Shapley-Shubik power index of each member and show that although the votes are in the ratio 1:1:2:3, the power indices are in the ratio 1:1:3:7. (Thus three votes are "worth" seven times a single vote and more than twice as much as two votes in this committee.)

3. To pass a motion, a bicameral legislature requires a majority vote in each house. House A has three and House B five members. Each legislator casts one vote.

   (a) Using symmetry considerations and the fact that the two houses have equal power, show that the Shapley-Shubik power index of each member of A is $1/6$ and of each member of B is $1/10$.

   (b) Verify the values obtained in part (a) by direct counting of voting orders, as required by the definition of the Shapley-Shubik power index.

4. Verify power indices for the protagonist coalition and for the other members, as entered in Table 1.

5. Krislov [20, p.463] makes the following claims in his study of power in a nine-person body.

   (i) "The 'swing man situation' so often discussed with regard to the Supreme Court offers the maximum payoff of .333 for an individual. That is to say, where two coalitions of four and four exist the ninth man may enter into decisions as effectively as either bloc."

(ii) "An example of intricacies of counter-organization is to be found in the 4,3,1,1 situation. Here counter-organization reduces the four-man power to .500 from .667. The three-man and the one-man coalitions equally share .167 of the power. Thus the three men actually slightly lower their payoff (formerly .200) by joining together, though they do succeed in transferring greater power from the dominant coalition to the independents."

Verify these claims.

6. To pass a bill, it must be voted for by the President and by a majority of each of two chambers, a three-person Senate and a five-person House.* Show that the Shapley-Shubik power index of the President is 32/84, of each Senator is 9/84, and of each House member is 5/84.

7. Consider a voting body of size n with each member casting one vote and w votes required to win. Suppose $w \geq (n+1)/2$. Show that the Shapley-Shubik power index of a coalition of x of these members is given by $x/(n-x+1)$ if $x \leq n-w+1$, by $(n-w+1)/(n-x+1)$ if $n-w+1 < x < w$, and by 1 if $w \leq x$.

8. A voting body of size 7 uses majority rule, as does one of its committees of size 3. To pass a proposal, both the committee and the entire body must vote approval. Calculate the Shapley-Shubik power index of each member of this body and show that the ratio of the power of a committee member to that of a non-committee member is 10:3. (This example is generalized in the next exercise.)

9. A faculty of size $2n+1$ uses majority rule, as does one of its committees of size $2m+1$. To pass a proposal requires approval of both the committee and the entire faculty. (Assume $n > 2m$ so a majority in the faculty is not automatic even if the committee supports an issue unanimously.) Verify the following assertions leading to a determination of the relative power of a committee member as compared to a non-committee member of the faculty.

(a) Each voting order of the $2n+1$ faculty members is one of $\binom{2n+1}{2m+1}$ different types, distinguished by the location in the ordering of the $2m+1$ committee members.

(b) A non-committee member is pivot in one of these ordering types if and only if he is preceded by exactly n faculty colleagues of whom at least $m+1$ are committee members. Hence, a non-committee member is pivot in a total of T orderings, where

$$T = \binom{n}{m+1}\binom{n}{m} + \binom{n}{m+2}\binom{n}{m-1} + \cdots + \binom{n}{2m+1}\binom{n}{0}.$$

*This example is worked out in Shapley and Shubik [45, p.792]. The Banzhaf theory is applied to this same example in Dubey and Shapley [13, p.103].

(c) Using the identity

$$\binom{2n}{k} = \sum_{j=0}^{k} \binom{n}{j}\binom{n}{k-j}$$

with $k = 2m + 1$ and breaking the sum into two parts (the first from $j = 0$ to $j = m$, the second from $j = m+1$ to $j = 2m+1$), note that the resulting sums are each equal to T. Hence

$$T = \tfrac{1}{2}\binom{2n}{2m+1}.$$

(d) The Shapley-Shubik power index of the non-committee members as a whole is $(n - m)/(2n + 1)$ and therefore the power index of the committee is $(n + m + 1)/(2n + 1)$.

(e) Let r denote the ratio of the size of the entire faculty to that of the committee. Then the ratio of the power of a committee member to that of a non-committee faculty colleague is $(1 + r){:}1$.

10. (a) Each member of a five-person voting body has one vote and majority rule applies. A lobbyist makes judgments about the "correctness" of each voter's position on a bill, a correct position being one that agrees with the lobbyist's. Suppose the voters act independently and each is correct with probability 0.6. What is the probability that the majority position of the entire voting body is correct?

(b) Suppose voters are no longer "equal" but that a weighted voting scheme exists in the body. For example, let votes be distributed as follows: (i) A and B each have 3 votes; C, D, E each have 1 vote; or (ii) A has five votes; B, C, D, E each have 1 vote. Note that a majority now requires at least 5 votes in (i) and (ii). Assuming the voters are still acting independently and that each casts a correct vote with probability 0.6, as in (a), determine for (i) and (ii) the new probability that the majority position of the body is correct.*

11. By filling in the details of the steps outlined below, prove the following result on majority rule:**

*This numerical example, considered by Weinstein [50], illustrates a general principle about majority rule. It is a corollary of a theorem due to Condorcet that if the probability of each voter being correct is greater than $1/2$, then it is more likely for the majority to be correct than it is for any single voter. See the discussion in Grofman [14].

**This result was conjectured by Rae [34] on the basis of some computations in the special case $p = 1/2$. Proofs were given by Schofield [41] and Taylor [49]. Curtis [9] generalized by allowing voters to have different probabilities of favoring the proposal, minimizing the average number of voters who find themselves on the losing side. Majority rule is also discussed by Straffin [47]. For the relation of this result to the Banzhaf power index, see Dubey and Shapley [13, p.106].

Theorem. Suppose an odd number, say n, of independent voters each has probability p $(p \sim 0, 1)$ of favoring a proposal and $q = 1 - p$ of voting against it. The proposal carries if and only if it receives at least k votes $(1 \leq k \leq n)$. Then the choice $k = (n+1)/2$, defining majority rule, minimizes each particular voter's chance of being on the losing side of the vote.

Step 1. A given voter is on the losing side in one of two ways:
(1) He votes "yes" and is joined by no more than $k - 2$ colleagues;
(2) He votes "no" and at least k of his colleagues vote "yes."
Thus the probability of the voter being on the losing side is

$$\sum_{i=0}^{k-2} \binom{n-1}{i} p^{i+1} q^{n-1-i} + \sum_{i=k}^{n} \binom{n-1}{i} p^i q^{n-i} = R(k), \text{ say.}$$

Step 2. To find the value of k that minimizes $R(k)$, first define $\Delta R(k) = R(k+1) - R(k)$ and show that

$$\Delta R(k) = p^k q^{n-k} \frac{(n-1)!}{k!(n-k)!} (2k - n).$$

Step 3. Note that $\Delta R(k) < 0$ if $k \leq (n-1)/2$ and $\Delta R(k) > 0$ if $k \geq (n+1)/2$, and thus complete the proof.

Bibliography

1. Banzhaf, J. F., "Weighted Voting Doesn't Work: A Mathematical Analysis," *Rutgers Law Review*, vol. 19 (1965), 317–343.
2. Banzhaf, J. F., "Multi-Member Electoral Districts—Do They Violate the 'One Man, One Vote' Principle?," *Yale Law Journal*, vol. 75 (1966), 1309–1338.
3. Banzhaf, J. F., "One Man, 3.312 Votes: A Mathematical Analysis of the Electoral College," *Villanova Law Review*, vol. 13 (1968), 304–332.
4. Banzhaf, J. F., "One Man, ? Votes: Mathematical Analysis of Political Consequences and Judicial Choices," *George Washington Law Review*, vol. 36 (1968), 808–823.
5. Ben-Dov, Y. and Y. Shilony, "Power and Importance in a Theory of Lobbying," *Behavioral Science*, vol. 27 (1982), 69–76.
6. Brams, S. J., *Game Theory and Politics*, New York: Free Press, 1975.
7. Coleman, J. S., "Control of Collectivities and the Power of the Collectivity to Act," pp.269–300 in Lieberman, B. (Ed.), *Social Choice*, London: Gordon and Breach, 1971.
8. Coleman, J. S., "Loss of Power," *American Sociological Review*, vol. 38 (1973), 1–17.

9. Curtis, R. B., "Decision Rules and Collective Values in Constitutional Choice," pp.23–33 in Niemi, R. G. and H. F. Weisberg (Eds.), *Probability Models of Collective Decision Making*, Columbus: Merrill, 1972.

10. Dahl, R. A., "The Concept of Power," *Behavioral Science*, vol. 2 (1957), 201–215.

11. Dahl, R. A., "Power," pp.405–415 in Sills, D. L. (Ed.), *International Encyclopedia of the Social Sciences*, vol. 12, New York: Crowell Collier and Macmillan, 1968. Reprinted in Wildavsky, A. (Ed.), *The Presidency*, Boston: Little, Brown, 1969.

12. David, P. T., R. M. Goldman, and R. C. Bain, *The Politics of National Party Conventions*, Washington D. C.: Brookings Institution, 1960.

13. Dubey, P. and L. S. Shapley, "Mathematical Properties of the Banzhaf Power Index," *Mathematics of Operations Research*, vol. 4 (1979), 99–131.

14. Grofman, B., "Judgemental Competence of Individuals and Groups in a Dichotomous Choice Situation: Is a Majority of Heads Better Than One?" *Journal of Mathematical Sociology*, vol. 6 (1978), 47–60.

15. Grofman, B., "Fair Apportionment and the Banzhaf Index," *American Mathematical Monthly*, vol. 88 (1981), 1–5.

16. Haefele, E., *Representative Government and Environmental Management*, Baltimore: Johns Hopkins University Press, 1973.

17. Imrie, R. W., "The Impact of the Weighted Vote on Representation in Municipal Governing Bodies of New York State," *Annals of the New York Academy of Sciences*, vol. 219 (1973), 192–199.

18. Johnson, R. E., "An Analysis of Weighted Voting as Used in Reapportionment of County Governments in New York State," *Albany Law Review*, vol. 34 (1969), 317–343.

19. Junn, R. S., "La Politique de l'Amendment des Articles 23 et 27 de la Charte des Nations Unies: Analyse Mathématique," *Mathématiques et Sciences Humaines*, vol. 40 (1972).

20. Krislov, S., "Power and Coalition in a Nine-Man Body," *American Behavioral Scientist*, vol. 6 (1963), 24–26. Reprinted (with corrections) in Schubert, G., *Judicial Behavior: a Reader in Theory and Research*, New York: Rand McNally, 1964.

21. Krislov, S., "The Power Index, Reapportionment and the Principle of One Man, One Vote," *Modern Uses of Logic in Law* (now *Jurimetrics*), (June 1965), 37–44.

22. Lucas, W. F., "Measuring Power in Weighted Voting Systems," pp.42–106 in C.U.P.M., *Case Studies in Applied Mathematics*, Washington, D. C.: Mathematical Association of America, 1976.

23. Luce, R. D. and H. Raiffa, *Games and Decisions*, New York: Wiley, 1957.

24. MacRae, D. and H. D. Price, "Scale Positions and 'Power' in the Senate," *Behavioral Science*, vol. 4 (1959), 212–218.

25. Mann, I. and L. S. Shapley, "The a priori Voting Strength of the Electoral College," pp.151–165 in Shubik, M. (Ed.), *Game Theory and Related Approaches to Social Behavior*, New York: Wiley, 1964.

26. March, J. G., "The Power of Power," pp.39–70 in Easton, D., *Varieties of Political Theory*, Englewood Cliffs: Prentice-Hall, 1966.

27. Merrill, S., "Citizen Voting Power Under the Electoral College: A Stochastic Model Based on State Voting Patterns," *SIAM Journal of Applied Mathematics*, vol. 34 (1978), 376–390.

28. Merrill, S., "Approximations to the Banzhaf Index of Voting Power," *American Mathematical Monthly*, vol. 89 (1982), 108–110.

29. Miller, D. R., "A Shapley Value Analysis of the Proposed Canadian Constitutional Amendment Scheme," *Canadian Journal of Political Science*, vol. 6 (1973), 140–143.

30. Monjardet, B., "Note sur les Pouvoirs de Vote au Conseil de Securité (A propos d'un Article de J. S. Junn)," *Mathématiques et Sciences Humaines*, vol. 40 (1972), 25–27.

31. Owen, G., *Game Theory*, second edition, New York: Academic Press, 1982.

32. Owen, G., "Political Games," *Naval Research Logistics Quarterly*, vol. 18 (1971), 345–355.

33. Owen, G., "Evaluation of a Presidential Election Game," *American Political Science Review*, vol. 69 (1975), 947–953 and vol. 70 (1976), 1223–1224.

34. Rae, D., "Decision-rules and Individual Values in Constitutional Choice," *American Political Science Review*, vol. 63 (1969), 40–56.

35. Rapoport, A., *N-Person Game Theory*, Ann Arbor: University of Michigan, 1970.

36. Riker, W. H., "A Test of the Adequacy of the Power Index," *Behavioral Science*, vol. 4 (1959), 120–131.

37. Riker, W. H., "Some Ambiguities in the Notion of Power," *American Political Science Review*, vol. 58 (1964), 341–349.

38. Riker, W. H. and D. Niemi, "The Stability of Coalitions on Roll Calls in the House of Representatives," *American Political Science Review*, vol. 54 (1962), 58–65.

39. Riker, W. H. and P. C. Ordeshook, *An Introduction to Positive Political Theory*, Englewood Cliffs: Prentice-Hall, 1973.

40. Riker, W. H. and L. S. Shapley, "Weighted Voting: A Mathematical Analysis for Instrumental Judgments," pp.199–216 in Pennock, J. R. and J. W. Chapman (Eds.), *Representation: Nomos X* (Yearbook of the American Society of Political and Legal Philosophy), New York: Atherton, 1968.

41. Schofield, N. J., "Is Majority Rule Special?" pp.60–82 in Neimi, R. G. and H. F. Weisberg (Eds.), *Probability Models of Collective Decision Making*, Columbus: Merrill, 1972.

42. Schubert, G., "The Power of Organized Minorities in a Small Group," *Administrative Science Quarterly*, vol. 9 (1964), 133–153. Reprinted in G. Schubert, *Judicial Behavior: A Reader in Theory and Research*, New York: Rand McNally, 1964.

43. Shapley, L. S., "A Value for N-Person Games," pp.307–317 in Kuhn, H. W. and A. W. Tucker (Eds.) *Contributions to the Theory of Games II*, Annals of Mathematics Studies No. 28, Princeton: Princeton University Press, 1953.

44. Shapley, L. S., *A Comparison of Power Indices and a Nonsymmetric Generalization*, P-5872, Santa Monica: the Rand Corporation, 1977.

45. Shapley, L. S. and M. Shubik, "A Method for Evaluating the Distribution of Power in a Committee System," *American Political Science Review*, vol. 48 (1954), 787–792.

46. Straffin, P. D., "Homogeneity, Independence and Power Indices," *Public Choice*, vol. 30 (1977), 107–118.

47. Straffin, P. D., "Majority Rule and General Decision Rules," *Theory and Decision*, vol. 8 (1977), 351–360.

48. Straffin, P. D., *Topics in the Theory of Voting*, Boston: Birkhäuser, 1980.

49. Taylor, M., "Proof of a Theorem on Majority Rule," *Behavioral Science*, vol. 14 (1969), 228–231.

50. Weinstein, J. B., "The Effect of Federal Reapportionment Decisions on Counties and Other Forms of Municipal Government," *Columbia Law Review*, vol. 65 (1965), 21–54.

51. Young, H. P., "Power, Prices and Incomes in Voting Systems," *Mathematical Programming*, vol. 14 (1978), 129–148.

Chapter 2
How Many People Have Ever Lived?

1. Introduction

Can the total number of people who have ever lived on the Earth be estimated in some reasonable way? This fascinating question has been the subject of a number of papers, the first by Winkler [15], others by Deevey [3], Desmond et al [4], Keyfitz [7], and the most recent by Westing [13]. Curiously enough, the two-page article by Keyfitz and the estimate obtained therein found their way into the Information Please Almanac [6] under the title "How Many Earth People Have There Been?"

These authors all assumed exponential growth during each of the time intervals between certain key dates at which times the total world population was taken to be known. We first show how deterministic exponential growth can be understood as the *average* behavior of a population whose size varies stochastically, growing over time due to the random occurrence of births and deaths. We then use the exponential growth model with some currently available data in order to answer the question posed in our title. Finally, we discuss the sensitivity of our estimate to various assumptions made along the way and compare our estimate with those obtained by others.

2. A Birth-Death Stochastic Process*

Let the number of persons alive at time t be a non-negative integer-valued random variable denoted by $N(t)$ and suppose

$$P_k(t) = P\big(N(t) = k\big) \qquad k = 0, 1, 2, \dots. \tag{1}$$

For each $t \geq 0$, these probabilities are non-negative and sum to 1, i.e.,

$$P_k(t) \geq 0, \qquad \sum_{k=0}^{\infty} P_k(t) = 1. \tag{2}$$

The assumption that the population size is initially fixed at i persons is expressed by the equations

$$P_i(0) = 1, \qquad P_k(0) = 0 \quad \text{if } k \sim i. \tag{3}$$

---

*Those who prefer on first reading to concentrate on the application to estimating world population can skip to Section 4.

We shall describe the so-called birth-death stochastic process, derive a system of differential-difference equations from which the probability distribution $P_k(t)$ can be calculated, and then show that the mean of this distribution can be determined *without* first calculating the distribution itself. This mean will turn out to be the familiar exponential function of elementary calculus describing exponential growth (if births overcome deaths) or exponential decay (if deaths overcome births).

We make two assumptions about the occurrence of births and deaths in a very small time interval of duration Δt (which will shortly be made to approach zero):

1. Each individual has probability $\lambda \Delta t$ to give birth (to a single offspring) and probability $\mu \Delta t$ to die in the elapsed time Δt. Here λ and μ are positive constants which measure the intensity of births and deaths, respectively. The larger λ (or μ), the more probable that a birth (or a death) occurs in the given time interval.

2. Births and deaths occur independently.

We note in passing that these assumptions ignore age and sex differences as well as multiple births, thus drastically oversimplifying the actual process of human population growth.*

To derive the fundamental equations from which the probabilities $P_k(t)$ can be determined, we need the following preliminary result.

Lemma. Let the size of the population be k at time t. In a small interval from t to $t + \Delta t$, the population can undergo transitions as follows:

$$\text{From } k \text{ persons, to } \begin{cases} k + 1 \text{ persons with probability } k\lambda\Delta t + o(\Delta t) \\ k - 1 \text{ persons with probability } k\mu\Delta t + o(\Delta t) \\ k \text{ persons with probability } 1 - k(\lambda + \mu)\Delta t + o(\Delta t) \\ k \pm n \ (n \geq 2) \text{ persons with probability } o(\Delta t). \end{cases}$$

Here $o(\Delta t)$ denotes any function of Δt that is of smaller order of magnitude than Δt. More precisely, a function $f(\Delta t)$ is said to be $o(\Delta t)$, read "little-oh of Δt" if

$$\frac{f(\Delta t)}{\Delta t} \to 0 \qquad \text{as } \Delta t \to 0.$$

Proof. If there are k persons alive at time t and each has probability $\lambda \Delta t$ to give birth and $\mu \Delta t$ to die in an elapsed time Δt, then there will be $k + 1$ persons at time $t + \Delta t$ provided either (i) exactly one of the k persons give birth and none of the k persons dies in the interval or (ii) exactly n $(2 \leq n \leq k)$ of the k persons give birth and $n - 1$ of the k persons die in

---

*One needs to start somewhere and it is a reasonable strategy to start with a very simple model. Although more complex and realistic assumptions can be made, this simple birth-death stochastic model turns out to have many applications and will suffice for our limited purpose in this unit. For more realistic models, see Keyfitz [8], and Pollard [11].

the interval. From the fact that we have k choices for the person who gives birth and using the independence assumption, we see that the probability of alternative (i) is given by*

$$k(\lambda\Delta t)(1 - \lambda\Delta t)^{k-1}(1 - \mu\Delta t)^k. \tag{4}$$

Expanding the binomials shows that this probability is equal to $k\lambda\Delta t$ plus terms with at least a factor $(\Delta t)^2$. These terms are each $o(\Delta t)$ and since the sum of a finite number of functions, each $o(\Delta t)$, is again $o(\Delta t)$, it follows that the probability of alternative (i) is $k\lambda\Delta t + o(\Delta t)$. Alternative (ii) has probability

$$\binom{k}{n}(\lambda\Delta t)^n(1 - \lambda\Delta t)^{k-n}\binom{k}{n-1}(\mu\Delta t)^{n-1}(1 - \mu\Delta t)^{k-n+1}. \tag{5}$$

Since $n \geq 2$, each term in this expansion has $(\Delta t)^3$ as a factor and hence is $o(\Delta t)$. Therefore alternative (ii) has probability $o(\Delta t)$ and it follows that the transition from k to $k + 1$ persons in the interval $(t, t + \Delta t)$ has probability $k\lambda\Delta t + o(\Delta t)$, as claimed. Similar arguments for the other possible transitions are used to complete the proof of the Lemma.

With this Lemma in hand, we turn to the derivation of equations satisfied by the probabilities $P_k(t)$. Consider the event, with probability $P_k(t + \Delta t)$, that $k \geq 1$ persons are alive at time $t + \Delta t$. We can obtain another expression for this probability by breaking up the event into the following mutually exclusive and exhaustive subevents determined by the number of persons alive at time t: for $n = 0, \pm 1, \pm 2, \ldots$, there are $k + n$ persons alive at time t and the transition from $k + n$ to k persons takes place in the interval from t to $t + \Delta t$. From the Lemma, the transition from k to k persons has probability $1 - k(\lambda + \mu)\Delta t + o(\Delta t)$; the transition from $k - 1$ to k persons has probability $(k - 1)\lambda\Delta t + o(\Delta t)$; the transition from $k + 1$ to k persons has probability $(k + 1)\mu\Delta t + o(\Delta t)$; the transition from a. population of any other starting size has probability $o(\Delta t)$. Hence, we see that

$$P_k(t + \Delta t) = P_k(t)\big(1 - k(\lambda+\mu)\Delta t + o(\Delta t)\big) + P_{k-1}(t)\big((k - 1)\lambda\Delta t + o(\Delta t)\big)$$
$$+ P_{k+1}(t)\big((k + 1)\mu\Delta t + o(\Delta t)\big) + o(\Delta t),$$

the final $o(\Delta t)$ being the aggregate contribution from populations with $k \pm 2$, $k \pm 3, \ldots$ persons at time t. (Note that we have used the fact that the

---

*Readers familiar with the binomial distribution will recognize (4) as the product of two binomial probabilities. The first is the probability of obtaining exactly one "success" (a birth) and therefore $k - 1$ "failures" (no births) in k Bernoulli trials with probability $\lambda\Delta t$ of a success in each trial. The second is the probability of obtaining zero "successes" (deaths) and therefore k "failures" (no deaths) on k Bernoulli trials with probability $\mu\Delta t$ of a success in each trial. A similar explanation can be made for the more general formula (5) which is the product of the binomial probabilities $\binom{k}{n}(\lambda\Delta t)^n(1 - \lambda\Delta t)^{k-n}$ and $\binom{k}{n-1}(\mu\Delta t)^{n-1}(1 - \mu\Delta t)^{k-n+1}$.

product of any factor not dependent on Δt and a function that is $o(\Delta t)$ is again $o(\Delta t)$.) Recalling that the sum of $o(\Delta t)$ terms is again $o(\Delta t)$, we obtain

$$P_k(t + \Delta t) = P_k(t) - k(\lambda + \mu)P_k(t)\Delta t + (k-1)\lambda P_{k-1}(t)\Delta t$$
$$+ (k+1)\mu P_{k+1}(t)\Delta t + o(\Delta t).$$

Transposing $P_k(t)$ to the left-hand side and dividing both sides of the resulting equation by Δt yields

$$\frac{P_k(t + \Delta t) - P_k(t)}{\Delta t} = -k(\lambda + \mu)P_k(t) + (k-1)\lambda P_{k-1}(t)$$
$$+ (k+1)\mu P_{k+1}(t) + \frac{o(\Delta t)}{\Delta t}.$$

Since $\frac{o(\Delta t)}{\Delta t} \to 0$ as $\Delta t \to 0$, the right-hand side has a limit as $\Delta t \to 0$. Hence so does the difference quotient on the left-hand side. But we recognize this limit as the derivative $\frac{dP_k(t)}{dt}$. Hence we have shown that for $k \geq 1$,

$$\frac{dP_k(t)}{dt} = -k(\lambda + \mu)P_k(t) + (k-1)\lambda P_{k-1}(t) + (k+1)\mu P_{k+1}(t). \quad (6)$$

If $k = 0$, a review of the just completed argument shows we need only exclude the impossible alternative that we start with -1 persons alive at time t. Otherwise the derivation proceeds unchanged and we obtain the equation

$$\frac{dP_0(t)}{dt} = \mu P_1(t). \quad (7)$$

The system of infinitely many differential-difference equations given by (6) and (7), together with the (infinitely many) initial conditions given by (3), can be solved* to determine the probability distribution $P_k(t)$ of the discrete random variable $N(t)$, the size of the population at time t. But we proceed instead to calculate the mean of this distribution directly from the differential-difference equations, without first solving them.

3.   Determination of the Mean Population Size

Let

$$m_1(t) = E[N(t)] = \sum_{k=0}^{\infty} k P_k(t)$$

and

$$m_2(t) = E[N^2(t)] = \sum_{k=0}^{\infty} k^2 P_k(t)$$

---

*See Chiang [2, p.272 ff.]

be the first moment (the mean) and the second moment, respectively, of the population size at time t. (Since the summands are zero for $k = 0$, note that we could equally well sum from $k = 1$. This fact is used below.) Now differentiating $m_1(t)$ and then substituting from (6), we have

$$\frac{d}{dt}m_1(t) = \sum_{k=1}^{\infty} k\frac{dP_k(t)}{dt}$$

$$= \sum_{k=1}^{\infty} k[-k(\lambda + \mu)P_k(t) + (k - 1)\lambda P_{k-1}(t) + (k + 1)\mu P_{k+1}(t)]$$

$$= -(\lambda + \mu)\sum_{k=1}^{\infty} k^2 P_k(t)$$

$$+ \lambda \sum_{k=1}^{\infty} k(k - 1)P_{k-1}(t) + \mu \sum_{k=1}^{\infty} k(k + 1)P_{k+1}(t).$$

To simplify the second and third sums on the right it is helpful to use the identities

$$k(k - 1) = (k - 1)^2 + (k - 1), \qquad k(k + 1) = (k + 1)^2 - (k + 1).$$

In the third sum let us also start from $k = 0$, which does not affect the sum but makes $k + 1$ vary from 1 to ∞. It is then easy to see that the equation for the derivative of $m_1(t)$ becomes

$$\frac{d}{dt}m_1(t) = -(\lambda + \mu)m_2(t) + \lambda[m_2(t) + m_1(t)] + \mu[m_2(t) - m_1(t)].$$

Since the second moment terms all cancel, we are left with

$$\frac{d}{dt}m_1(t) = (\lambda - \mu)m_1(t), \qquad (8)$$

the familiar differential equation for exponential growth (if $\lambda > \mu$) or exponential decay (if $\lambda < \mu$).

Letting $\lambda - \mu = r$ be the net growth factor, the general solution of this differential equation is

$$m_1(t) = ce^{rt} \qquad (9)$$

where c is an arbitrary constant. Using the initial conditions (3), we see that $m_1(0) = i$ so that $c = i$, the initial population size, but we shall not need this fact. In the next section we simply assume exponential growth, although we now realize that this pattern of growth can be interpreted in two different ways:

(i) the population grows *deterministically* and its *actual size* at any time t follows the exponential path given by (9);

(ii) the population grows *stochastically* according to a birth-death probabilistic process, its size at any time t is therefore a random variable, but its *mean or average size* at time t grows exponentially as given by (9).

It may be helpful to think of these interpretations in the following way. Let us observe a large number of different populations, each undergoing exponential growth with the same values of the parameters c and r. In the deterministic model, at each moment of time, all the populations would have the same size, as given by (9). But in the stochastic model we would expect to see variation from one population to the next, with different populations having different sizes at any given moment. However, the *average size* of these populations at any time t would be approximately given by equation (9), the approximation tending to improve the larger the number of populations whose sizes are averaged.

4. Fitting an Exponential Curve

Let us now simplify matters and write $n(t)$ for the number of persons living at time t. Suppose we know (or guess) this number at two different dates, say t_1 and t_2. Say $n(t_1) = n_1$ and $n(t_2) = n_2$, identifying the two points A and B in Figure 1.

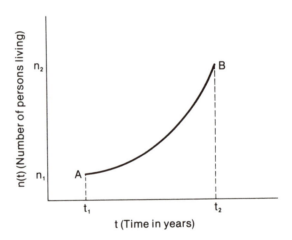

Figure 1. Exponential curve passing through two points.

The key assumption that population size has grown *exponentially* during the time from t_1 to t_2 means that positive constants c and r exist so that for $t_1 \leq t \leq t_2$,

$$n(t) = ce^{rt}. \tag{10}$$

This is, of course, the equation derived and interpreted in the preceding section. Although we now adopt the simpler language of the deterministic interpretation, a reader can choose to think of $n(t)$ as the *mean* number of persons living at time t for a population growing stochastically according to a birth-death probability process. Since we want the particular exponential curve passing through points A and B, the constants c and r in (10) are determined by the two conditions

$$n(t_1) = n_1 \quad \text{and} \quad n(t_2) = n_2,$$

from which

$$n_1 = ce^{rt_1} \quad \text{and} \quad n_2 = ce^{rt_2}. \tag{11}$$

Dividing yields

$$\frac{n_2}{n_1} = e^{r(t_2 - t_1)} \tag{12}$$

and taking logarithms,

$$r = \frac{\ln(n_2) - \ln(n_1)}{t_2 - t_1}. \tag{13}$$

With this value of r in the first of the equations (11) we have

$$c = n_1 e^{-rt_1}$$

and so, from (10)

$$n(t) = n_1 e^{r(t - t_1)}. \tag{14}$$

With r specified by (13), this is the unique exponential curve passing through the points A and B in Figure 1.

The total person-years lived from time t_1 to time t_2 is given by the area under the exponential curve above the interval (t_1, t_2), i.e., by the integral

$$\int_{t_1}^{t_2} n_1 e^{r(t - t_1)} \, dt = \frac{n_1}{r}(e^{r(t_2 - t_1)} - 1)$$

$$= \frac{n_1(t_2 - t_1)}{\ln(n_2) - \ln(n_1)}\left(\frac{n_2}{n_1} - 1\right),$$

substituting from (12) and (13). Simplifying yields the final formula

$$\text{Person-years lived in } (t_1, t_2) = \frac{(n_2 - n_1)(t_2 - t_1)}{\ln(n_2) - \ln(n_1)}. \tag{15}$$

Of course, this assumes $n_1 \sim n_2$ (see Exercise 4). The approximate number of persons who lived in (t_1, t_2) is then obtained by dividing the person-years lived by the average life expectancy for that time period.

5.   Population Data and Results

Formula (15) is used for each of a number of time intervals into which we divide the time span from the first human presence to today. The estimate we end up with will depend on our choice of this first date and on the way this time span is subdivided into smaller intervals in each of which the method requires the fitting of an exponential growth curve. Let us begin with an extremely coarse estimate obtained by using a single time interval starting with 1,500,000 years before the Christian Era and ending with the year 1980. For $t_1 = -1,500,000$ years we take $n_1 = 2$ persons and for $t_2 = 1980$ years we take $n_2 = 4,400,000,000$.* Applying Formula (15), we obtain 307×10^{12} person-years and after dividing by 25 (which we take as an average life expectancy), an estimated 12 trillion people. (Such computations and those required below are done in a few minutes using a computer or a scientific hand-held calculator.)

It is more reasonable to divide this single large time span into a number of smaller subintervals by using times for which estimates of world population have been made.** In Keyfitz and Flieger [9, p.viii] we find the following:

It took ... up to 8000 B.C. to attain a population of five millions in the world.

... about the reign of Julius Caesar 300 million people, to within a hundred million either way, were dispersed over the planet. A similar pace of growth ... continued through the Middle Ages and after, so that by 1750 A.D. the total was about 800 millions.

But now an acceleration started. The first billion was reached about 1825; the second billion about 1925; the third billion about 1960.

These data, together with our assumed starting population and time and the United Nations estimate of 1980 world population, are summarized in Table 1 on the next page.

In the last column of Table 1 we have the results of using Formula (15) for each of the seven time intervals. The total person-years adds to 2.367×10^{12}. Dividing by an assumed average expectation of life of 25 years, we obtain an estimate of 94.7×10^9 or about 95 billion for the number of

---

*Keyfitz [7] starts with Adam and Eve at $t = -1,000,000$ years and ends with 3 billion persons in 1960. Westing's [13] starting date of 298,000 B.C. is based on estimates of when *Homo sapiens* first appeared on Earth. The dividing line between man and ape is still a matter of anthropological controversy, but *Homo habilis*, dated about 1,500,000 years ago, may as well be our starting point in this very rough approximation. The world population figure used for 1980 is given by the United Nations [12, Table 1]. Our estimate of 12 trillion is reduced by about a factor of five if the single time interval is taken to start with Westing's 298,000 B.C. Either way, the estimate obtained in this simple-minded fashion is ridiculously high.

**These estimates, even for recent years, can only be rough approximations. As one goes back in time, a growing margin for error must be allowed. The reliability of historical population estimates and assumptions on which they are based are surveyed by Durand [5] and Biraben [1].

Year of Christian Era t	World Population n	$\ln n$	$\dfrac{(n_2 - n_1)(t_2 - t_1)}{\ln(n_2) - \ln(n_1)}$
−1,500,000	2	0.693	
−8,000	5,000,000	15.425	$.506 \times 10^{12}$
−50	300,000,000	19.519	$.573 \times 10^{12}$
1750	800,000,000	20.500	$.918 \times 10^{12}$
1825	1,000,000,000	20.723	$.067 \times 10^{12}$
1925	2,000,000,000	21.416	$.144 \times 10^{12}$
1960	3,000,000,000	21.822	$.086 \times 10^{12}$
1980	4,400,000,000	22.205	$.073 \times 10^{12}$
			2.367×10^{12}

Table 1. Calculation of total person-years based on seven time intervals.

persons who have lived on the Earth. (It is true that we could use different average life expectancies for each of the subintervals of time to reflect changing conditions, but as we shall see the result is not very sensitive to these numbers and such additional precision is difficult to justify in light of the rough population estimates used in our calculations.)

It is easy to see why this estimate, based on seven exponential curves, one fitted over each of the seven time intervals in Table 1, is so much lower than the 12 trillion people obtained on the basis of one exponential curve fitted to the two end points of the time span. The single exponential joins the two points given by $t_1 = -1,500,000$, $n_1 = 2$ and $t_2 = 1980$, $n_2 = 4,400,000,000$. Using these values we determine $r = .00001432$ from (13) and then from (14) we can compute the height of this exponential at any intermediate time t. For example, we find

$$n(-8000) = 3,810,000,000$$
$$n(-50) = 4,270,000,000$$
$$n(1750) = 4,390,000,000, \text{ etc.}$$

These are significantly larger than the corresponding population sizes entered in Table 1 and so the area under each of the seven fitted exponentials is much smaller than the area above the same time interval under the single exponential curve.

How does our final value of 95 billion humans who have inhabited the Earth at one time or another compare with estimates obtained by others? Westing [13] gets 50 billion using different key dates (but still numbering eight in all) and starting with 298,000 B.C.* He also uses an average life expectancy that varies from a low of 20 years to a high (during his most

---

*He makes a computational error. The correct total based on his data is 46.4 billion. See Exercise 5.

recent interval from 1945 to 1980) of 50 years. The estimate of Keyfitz [7], when his five key dates (from 1,000,000 B.C. to 1960) are augmented by a sixth for 1980, becomes 72 billion. He assumes a constant 25-year life expectancy over all periods. Desmond [4], starts with 600,000 B.C. and uses three intervals, obtaining an estimate of 77 billion up to the year 1962. Using twelve time periods starting with the Lower Paleolithic of some one million years ago, Deevey [3, p.197] concludes that "about 110 billion individuals seem to have passed their days, and left their bones, if not their marks, on this crowded planet." Finally, we have repeated our calculations based on 30 key dates and world population estimates* (26 of these, ranging from 400 B.C. to 1970, are from Biraben [1, Table 2], and four others, 298,000 B.C., 40,000 B.C., 8,000 B.C., and 1980, are used by Westing), and also assuming a fixed life expectancy of 25 years. The result, using this much finer subdivision of the total time from 298,000 B.C. to 1980, was a total of 62 billion. This total rises to 72 billion if one starts with two people at 1,500,000 B.C. instead of at 298,000 B.C. Introducing the additional variation in life expectancy, as in Westing, from a low of 20 years in the earliest period to a high of 50 years in the latest decades, these totals become 46 and 60 billion, respectively.

It appears that a range from 50 to 100 billion is a reasonable estimate for the answer to the question posed in our title. It is interesting to note that the approximately 4.4 billion persons inhabiting the Earth in 1980 make up somewhere between 4% and 9% of the number who ever lived. The upper value of 9% seemed startling enough to be featured in a recent headline in the *New York Times* [14].

Exercises

1. Modify the birth-death process in the text by supposing $\mu = 0$, i.e., eliminate deaths. The result is the so-called Yule birth process. Let us assume an initial population size of 1.

   (a) Reformulate the Lemma of the text to show that in a small time interval from t to $t + \Delta t$ the population can undergo transitions as follows:

Transition	Probability
$k \to k+1$	$k\lambda\Delta t + o(\Delta t)$
$k \to k$	$1 - k\lambda\Delta t + o(\Delta t)$
$k \to k+n \quad (n \geq 2)$	$o(\Delta t).$

---

*In this finer subdivision of time, there are time periods during which there was a *decline* of world population. The outbreak of the plague caused total world population to decline from 443 million in 1340 to 374 million in 1400. See the discussion of such phases of growth and decline in Biraben [1, pp.9–12].

(b) Show that $P_0(t) = 0$ for all t and

$$\frac{dP_k(t)}{dt} = -k\lambda P_k(t) + (k-1)\lambda P_{k-1}(t) \qquad k = 1, 2, \ldots . \quad (16)$$

(c) Put $k = 1$ in (16), solve the resulting differential equation, and thus show that $P_1(t) = e^{-\lambda t}$.

(d) Put $k = 2$ in (16), use (c), and solve the resulting equation to show that $P_2(t) = e^{-\lambda t}(1 - e^{-\lambda t})$.

(e) Use mathematical induction to prove that

$$P_k(t) = e^{-\lambda t}(1 - e^{-\lambda t})^{k-1} \qquad k = 1, 2, \ldots .$$

(f) Show that $E[N(t)] = e^{\lambda t}$ and $\text{Var}[N(t)] = e^{\lambda t}(e^{\lambda t} - 1)$ for the Yule process.

2. (a) Show directly from the system of differential-difference equations (6) that $m_2(t)$, the second moment of the random population size $N(t)$, satisfies the differential equation

$$\frac{dm_2(t)}{dt} + 2(\mu - \lambda)m_2(t) = (\lambda + \mu)ie^{(\lambda-\mu)t}$$

where i is the initial population size at time 0.

(b) Noting that $e^{2(\mu-\lambda)t}$ is an integrating factor, solve the differential equation to find (if $\lambda \sim \mu$)

$$m_2(t) = (i^2 + i\frac{\lambda+\mu}{\lambda-\mu})e^{2(\lambda-\mu)t} - i\frac{\lambda+\mu}{\lambda-\mu}e^{(\lambda-\mu)t}.$$

(c) Recalling that the variance of $N(t)$ is given by

$$\text{Var}[N(t)] = m_2(t) - [m_1(t)]^2,$$

show that (if $\lambda \sim \mu$)

$$\text{Var}[N(t)] = i\frac{\lambda+\mu}{\lambda-\mu}e^{(\lambda-\mu)t}(e^{(\lambda-\mu)t} - 1).$$

(d) Suppose $\lambda = \mu$, i.e., the net growth rate $r = \lambda - \mu = 0$. Use L'Hospital's rule (or otherwise) show that $\text{Var}[N(t)] = 2i\lambda t$.

3. Consult Chiang [2], Pielou [10] or some other book on stochastic processes to learn how to obtain the explicit solution of the system of differential-difference equations (6) that govern the birth-death process. Also, look into the determination of the probability of the ultimate extinction of the population, i.e., $\lim_{t \to \infty} P_0(t)$. The result, assuming initial population size i, is as follows:

$$\lim_{t \to \infty} P_0(t) = \begin{cases} 1 & \text{if } \lambda \leq \mu \\ (\mu/\lambda)^i & \text{if } \lambda > \mu. \end{cases}$$

In words: if $\lambda \leq \mu$, then extinction is certain; if $\lambda > \mu$, then extinction occurs with probability only $(\mu/\lambda)^i$. The result when $\lambda = \mu$ is especially interesting since in this case $m_1(t) = i$ so the mean population size stays fixed at i persons for all time. But the variance of the population size grows linearly with time (as shown in Exercise 2(d)) and ultimate extinction turns out to be an event that occurs with probability 1.

4. (a) Show that formula (15) for the person-years lived in (t_1, t_2) can be written as $(n_2 - n_1)/r$ if $r \sim 0$ and as $n_1(t_2 - t_1)$ if $r = 0$.

(b) Assuming exponential growth as in equation (14), show that the size of the population doubles in $(\ln 2)/r$ years. Using the data in Table 1 for the period from 1960 to 1980, show that the doubling time for the world population is about 36 years. Compute the doubling time over the six earlier periods in Table 1.

5. Westing [13] uses the data in Table 2 to obtain his estimate of 50 billion humans who have ever lived on the Earth. Determine the total number of person-years lived and the total number of persons born in each of the seven intervals into which the period from 298,000 B.C. to 1980 is subdivided. Show that Westing's total should be about 46 billion. (His Table 3 includes a calculating error leading to the reporting of 17.7 instead of the correct 14.1 million persons born in the period from 8000 B.C. to 0.)

Date	World Population	Life Expectancy (Years)
298,000 B.C.	2	20
40,000 B.C.	3,000,000	25
8,000 B.C.	5,000,000	30
0	200,000,000	35
1650	500,000,000	40
1850	1,000,000,000	45
1945	2,300,000,000	50
1980	4,400,000,000	

Table 2. World population from Westing [13].

6. Using the data in Table 1 and a fixed 25-year life expectancy, the 4.4 billion persons alive in 1980 represent just under 5% of the 95 billion persons who have ever lived on the Earth. Extend the calculations to the year 2000 by using $n(1990) = 5.3 \times 10^9$ and $n(2000) = 6.2 \times 10^9$, as estimated by the United Nations [12]. Thus show that the 6.2 billion persons alive in 2000 will make up almost 9% of the 99 billion persons who will have ever lived on the Earth by that time.

Bibliography

1. Biraben, J. N., "An Essay Concerning Mankind's Evolution," *Population Selected Papers No. 4* (Dec. 1980), 1–13; translated from *Population*, vol. 34 (1979), 13–25.
2. Chiang, C. L., *An Introduction to Stochastic Processes and Their Applications*, Huntington, N. Y.: Krieger, 1980.
3. Deevey, E. S. Jr., "The Human Population," *Scientific American*, vol. 203 (Sept. 1960), 194–204.
4. Desmond, A., *et al*, "How Many People Have Ever Lived On Earth?," *Population Bulletin*, vol. XVIII (Feb. 1962), 1–19.
5. Durand, J. D., "Historical Estimates of World Population: An Evaluation," *Population and Development Review*, vol. 3 (1977), 253–296.
6. *Information Please Almanac 1974*, New York: Simon & Schuster, 1973.
7. Keyfitz, N., "How Many People Have Lived On The Earth?," *Demography*, vol. 3 (1966), 581–582.
8. Keyfitz, N., *Introduction to the Mathematics of Population*, Reading Mass.: Addison-Wesley, 1968.
9. Keyfitz, N. and W. Flieger, *World Population: An Analysis of Vital Data*, Chicago: University of Chicago Press, 1968.
10. Pielou, E. C., *An Introduction to Mathematical Ecology*, New York: Wiley, 1969.
11. Pollard, J. H., *Mathematical Models for the Growth of Human Populations*, London: Cambridge University Press, 1973.
12. UN Dept. Int'l. Econ. & Soc. Affairs, Publication no. ST/ESA/SER.A/70, *World Population Trends and Policies*, 1979 Monitoring Report, vol. 1 (Population Trends), New York: United Nations, 1980.
13. Westing, A. H., "A Note On How Many Humans That Have Ever Lived," *BioScience*, vol. 31 (July–Aug. 1981), 523–524. See also "A New Grand, Grand Population Total," *Intercom*, vol. 9 (Oct. 1981), 6 and the Correction in *Intercom*, vol. 9 (Nov./Dec. 1981), 14.
14. Wilford, J. N., "9 Percent Of Everyone Who Ever Lived Is Alive Now," *The New York Times*, October 6, 1981, p.C1.
15. Winkler, W., "Wieviele Menschen haben bisher auf der Erde gelebt?," pp.73–76 in *International Population Conference, Vienna 1959*, Vienna: Union Internationale pour l'Etude Scientifique de la Population, 1959.

Chapter 3
Management of Research Projects

1. Introduction

Problems involved in planning and managing research and development projects have been studied by a number of investigators. The probabilistic models they have constructed are generally considered a part of operations research or managerial economics. We formulate and solve two such problems here. In addition to illustrating the use of ideas and techniques from probability theory, they also serve as vehicles for the introduction of some important ideas of dynamic programming (Problem 1) and of discounting and present value of cash flows (Problem 2).

Problem 1 concerns the allocation of money from a limited budget in order to fund alternative independent proposals for achieving a given objective. The idea of management trying to maximize the probability of achieving the project objective by supporting more than one competing proposal, of building redundancy into what is funded, assuming the budget allows such multiple efforts, is reasonable enough. Note the distinction between this managerial goal (achieve the objective, one way or another) and the more complex goal, for example, in managing a portfolio of stocks in order to maximize expected return. In Problem 1, one successful proposal achieves management's objective even if other funded proposals do not pan out. But one "successful" stock in a portfolio is not sufficient cause for rejoicing since the performance of the other stocks in the portfolio cannot be ignored.

Problem 2 develops a simple version of a model to guide a company's decision on whether or not to initiate a project and, once started, whether to continue it to completion or shut it down if it hasn't been successfully concluded after a certain length of time. Balancing is required of the potential monetary gain to be earned upon successful completion against the anticipated costs of continued operation. Both this gain and operating costs are assumed known, and simplifying (and somewhat unrealistic) assumptions about these quantities are imposed to make the problem tractable. Randomness is introduced by treating the project completion time as a chance variable.

2. Problem 1

Suppose a new foundation or research institute has a specific project objective (finding a cure for some disease, for example) and has received proposals

33

from a number of different teams of researchers who suggest different and independent technical alternatives for accomplishing the objective. (One team suggests research with viruses, another with controlled diets, another with preventive drug treatment, etc.)   Each alternative has assigned to it a probability of being successful in achieving the objective as well as a cost for carrying it out. The foundation or institute has budgeted a certain total amount of money for funding one or more of these alternatives and naturally wishes to do so in such a way that it maximizes the probability of achieving its project objective. How should it allocate funds to the various research teams who have submitted proposals?

Let us introduce symbols as follows:

p_i = probability that alternative i is successful if funded,

c_i = cost of carrying out alternative i,

B = total amount (in \$) budgeted (i.e., available to be allocated) for this project.

Of course, $i = 1, 2, \ldots, n$ where n is the number of independent alternatives seeking support. *For each positive integer n we wish to know which alternatives to support, within the total allowable budget of \$B, so the probability of achieving the project objective is maximized.* Our procedure is to divide the problem into stages, solving each successive stage until we have a complete solution. In stage 1 we will pretend to have only alternative 1 available; in stage 2 we will have alternatives 1 and 2; in stage 3 we consider alternatives 1, 2, and 3; etc. At each stage, we seek an optimal choice of alternatives, optimal in the sense of making the probability of achieving the project objective as large as possible, conditional on the available alternatives and, of course, satisfying the total cost constraint. Let us define $f_i(B)$ as this *maximum probability of achieving the project objective for an optimal set of alternatives chosen from the first i alternatives when the total amount budgeted for the project is \$B.*

For $i = 1$ we have only alternative 1 to consider and so the best policy is clear: fund alternative 1, but only if it can be afforded. In symbols:

$$f_1(B) = \begin{cases} p_1 & \text{if } c_1 \leq B \\ 0 & \text{if } c_1 > B. \end{cases}$$

Next we move to stage $i = 2$. If c_2, the cost of alternative 2, exceeds the total available money B, then we clearly can do no better than the best we could do with just alternative 1, i.e.,

$$f_2(B) = f_1(B) \qquad \text{if } c_2 > B.$$

But if $c_2 \leq B$ we must consider the possibility that funding alternative 2 is worthwhile. So we compare the probabilities of achieving our objective under two plans:

Plan 1. Fund alternative 2 first and then (having reduced the problem to stage 1), fund alternative 1 if sufficient money still remains.

Plan 2. Do not fund alternative 2 and do the best we can considering only alternative 1 (a stage 1 problem).

Of course, since our aim is to maximize the probability of achieving the objective, we will choose the plan with the larger probability. With Plan 2 we know the best we can do yields the probability $f_1(B)$. With Plan 1 the probability of achieving the objective (i.e., having *at least one* of the two alternatives result in success) is most easily computed by subtracting from 1 the probability that both alternatives will fail. The probability that alternative 2 fails is $1 - p_2$. Since we have now spent c_2 dollars, only $B - c_2$ remain. With this amount available and only alternative 1 to consider, the best probability of success is known from stage 1 to be $f_1(B - c_2)$. Hence, since we assumed independence of alternatives, the probability that both alternatives fail is $(1 - p_2)(1 - f_1(B - c_2))$. Subtracting this product from 1 gives the probability of achieving the objective under Plan 1. Denoting the larger of the two numbers a and b by $\text{Max}[a, b]$, we can summarize our argument by writing the following solution for the stage 2 problem:

$$f_2(B) = \begin{cases} \text{Max}[1 - (1 - p_2)(1 - f_1(B - c_2)), \ f_1(B)] & \text{if } c_2 \leq B \\ f_1(B) & \text{if } c_2 > B. \end{cases}$$

Note the way this stage 2 solution used the previously obtained solution for stage 1. And we continue in this sequential manner, the derivation for any stage making the same use of the preceding stage solution that the stage 2 derivation made of the stage 1 solution. The result for n alternative research proposals (stage n) can be summarized as follows:

$$f_n(B) = \begin{cases} \text{Max}[1 - (1 - p_n)(1 - f_{n-1}(B - c_n)), \ f_{n-1}(B)] & \text{if } c_n \leq B \\ f_{n-1}(B) & \text{if } c_n > B. \end{cases}$$

To illustrate the use of these recursive equations, consider a problem with three independent proposals for achieving the research objective and with probabilities and costs given by

$$p_1 = .7 \qquad p_2 = .3 \qquad p_3 = .6$$
$$c_1 = 4 \qquad c_2 = 1 \qquad c_3 = 3.$$

Some sample calculations:

$$f_2(B) = \begin{cases} \text{Max}[1 - (1 - .3)(1 - f_1(B - 1)), \ f_1(B)] & \text{if } 1 \leq B \\ f_1(B) & \text{if } 1 > B, \end{cases}$$

from which, since $f_1(B) = .7$ if $4 \leq B$ and $f_1(B) = 0$ if $4 > B$,

$$f_2(2) = \text{Max}[1 - (.7)(1 - 0), \ 0] = .3,$$
$$f_2(3) = \text{Max}[1 - (.7)(1 - 0), \ 0] = .3,$$
$$f_2(4) = \text{Max}[1 - (.7)(1 - 0), \ .7] = .7,$$
$$f_2(5) = \text{Max}[1 - (.7)(1 - .7), \ .7] = .79, \text{ etc.}$$

Finally,

$$f_3(B) = \begin{cases} \text{Max}[1 - (1 - .6)(1 - f_2(B - 3)), f_2(B)] & \text{if } 3 \le B \\ f_2(B) & \text{if } 3 > B, \end{cases}$$

from which

$$f_3(2) = f_2(2) = .3,$$
$$f_3(3) = \text{Max}[1 - (.4)(1), .3] = .6,$$
$$f_3(4) = \text{Max}[1 - (.4)(.7), .7] = .72,$$
$$\cdots$$
$$f_3(7) = \text{Max}[1 - (.4)(.3), .79] = .88,$$
$$f_3(8) = \text{Max}[1 - (.4)(.21), .79] = .916, \text{ etc.}$$

From these maximum probabilities $f_i(B)$ we also automatically determine whether or not to fund a particular alternative. For example, consider the stage 3 probabilities and suppose $B = 7$. The maximum value of the two probabilities used to compute $f_3(7)$ is the first probability, the one corresponding to Plan 1. We conclude that alternative 3 *is* funded. This leaves us with $B - c_3 = 7 - 3 = 4$ as available funds for stage 2. In computing $f_2(4)$, the maximum value is the Plan 2 probability and so alternative 2 is *not* funded and we still are left with available funds equal to 4 for stage 1, just sufficient to fund alternative 1. So with $B = 7$, the optimal choice is to fund only alternatives 1 and 3 and this produces a maximum probability equal to $f_3(7) = .88$ for achieving the research objective. Of course, if $B \ge 8$ then all three alternatives should be funded and the maximum probability of achieving the objective rises to .916.

Total Budget B	Alternative 1 $p_1 = .7, c_1 = 4$		Alternative 2 $p_2 = .3, c_2 = 1$		Alternative 3 $p_3 = .6, c_3 = 3$	
	Fund?	$f_1(B)$	Fund?	$f_2(B)$	Fund?	$f_3(B)$
0	no	0	no	0	no	0
1	no	0	yes	.3	no	.3
2	no	0	yes	.3	no	.3
3	no	0	yes	.3	yes	.6
4	yes	.7	no	.7	yes	.72
5	yes	.7	yes	.79	no	.79
6	yes	.7	yes	.79	no	.79
7	yes	.7	yes	.79	yes	.88
8	yes	.7	yes	.79	yes	.916

Table 1. Summary of optimal decisions for illustrative example.

Table 1 summarizes all such decisions and calculations and can be used to read the solution to our illustrative problem for any total budgeted amount B. For example, we can easily verify our previously obtained solution when $B = 7$. Starting at the $B = 7$ row and the alternative 3 column, we read "yes" so alternative 3 is funded at its cost of $c_3 = 3$ and with $f_3(7) = .88$. Now we have $B - c_3 = 4$ left in available funds, so going across the row with cost 4 we read "no" under the alternative 2 heading. Hence alternative 2 is not funded and we move to the left in the same row, find a "yes" in the alternative 1 column, and thus conclude, as before, that with $B = 7$ the maximum probability of achieving the objective is .88 and alternative proposals 1 and 3 are funded in order to reach this best chance of success.

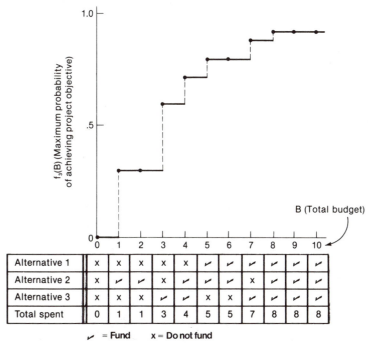

Figure 1. Optimal decisions and probabilities for illustrative example.

Figure 1 is a graphical representation of our solution for this illustrative example. It makes clear the way the maximum probability of achieving the project objective varies (from 0 to .916) with the total amount budgeted for the project. Appearing below each value of the total budget B are other features of the optimal solution: the alternatives to be funded and the total amount actually spent.

Larger problems, with many more alternatives, could be solved in a similar fashion although the number of calculations becomes burdensome. But the recursive nature of the solution makes it particularly suited for a high-speed computer and one can program such a computer to produce a general summary of results like Table 1 or a solution for one or more special problems with particular values of B. We thus have a practical method of determining the optimal set of alternative research proposals that should be supported and the maximum probability of achieving the research objective as a function of the number of proposed alternatives and the total funds available.

3. Problem 2

A company is presented at some time (which we take to be $t = 0$) with a proposal for a research project. Implementing this project requires continuous company expenditures at a constant rate of c (in dollars, say) per year. The completion time for the project depends on many uncontrollable factors and is assumed to be a positive random variable T (years) with a known cumulative distribution function F and probability density function f. That is, we have

$$\Pr(a < T < b) = \int_a^b f(t)\,dt \qquad (b > a \geq 0)$$

and

$$F(x) = \Pr(T \leq x) = \int_0^x f(t)\,dt \qquad (x \geq 0).$$

If the project is completed, there is a return to the company (valued at the moment of completion) of R dollars.

The problem is to decide on the company policy: Is it worth undertaking the research project? Once undertaken, should it be continued until completion or should it be shut down if it hasn't been concluded after a certain length of time?

In order to approach these questions we need to decide on a method by which our company will measure the investment worth of a given course of action involving both income received and expenditures paid out over time. Money and other resources used by the company are not free. After all, money could be used to earn interest in a bank account or be invested to earn a return in some other venture. Suppose money earns interest at the compound annual rate $100r\%$ and is compounded n times per year. Then A dollars today amounts to

$$A\left(1 + \frac{r}{n}\right)^{nt}$$

dollars after t years since the interest rate per conversion period is $100r/n$ percent and there are nt compoundings in the t years. As $n \to \infty$, i.e., as interest is compounded more and more frequently, the amount after t years increases to Ae^{rt} since

$$\lim_{n\to\infty}\left(1 + \frac{r}{n}\right)^n = e^r.$$

We say that Ae^{rt} is the amount resulting after t years from an initial investment of A under *continuous compounding* at the rate 100r% per year. We shall adopt continuous compounding and use the symbol r to specify the applicable annual interest rate, assumed to stay the same for the duration of the project. Of course, it follows that if an amount A dollars is received t years in the future, it is *discounted* to the present by multiplication by e^{-rt} and we refer to Ae^{-rt} as its *present value.*

We assume the company uses net present value as its measure of investment worth. Having decided on an appropriate interest rate, company executives compute the present value of the cash inflow from the investment minus the present value of the cash outflow. If this difference, the so-called *net present value of the project*, is positive then the investment opportunity is accepted and the project starts. If the net present value of the project is negative or zero, the opportunity is rejected.

There is a complication in our problem due to the fact that the net present value of the project, depending as it does on the random completion time T, is itself a random variable. In this case, we determine the mean or expectation of the net present value and adopt as company policy the following decision rule: *Accept the proposal and let the project start if its mean net present value is positive; otherwise reject the proposal.*

We now turn to the analysis needed to implement this decision rule. Denote by $v_0(T)$ the net present value at time 0 of the project carried out to completion at time T. We must discount back to time 0 all costs and returns. The return R obtained at completion time T has present value Re^{-rT} at $t = 0$. The stream of cash outlays at the rate c per unit time and occurring continuously throughout the time interval $(0, T)$ has present value given by the integral*

$$\int_0^T ce^{-rt}\, dt$$

which, when evaluated, equals $(c/r)(1 - e^{-rT})$. Hence

$$v_0(T) = e^{-rT}(R + \frac{c}{r}) - \frac{c}{r}. \qquad (1)$$

Since T is actually a random variable, so is $v_0(T)$. We therefore base our decision on

$$w(0) = E[v_0(T)],$$

---

*Divide the interval $(0, T)$ into n equal subintervals, each of length Δt. The cash outlay in each subinterval is $c\Delta t$. If t_i is an arbitrary point selected in the ith subinterval, then $c\Delta te^{-rt_i}$ is approximately the discounted value of the outlays made in the ith subinterval. And $\sum_{i=1}^{n} ce^{-rt_i}\Delta t$ is approximately the present value of all outlays made in the entire interval $(0, T)$. In the limit, as the number of subintervals increases without bound, this (Riemann) sum approaches the integral $\int_0^T ce^{-rt}\, dt$, which is taken as the present value of the continuous outlays over $(0, T)$.

the *mean* (or expectation) of the net present value of the project at time 0. Since T has density function f,

$$w(0) = \int_0^\infty v_0(s)f(s)\,ds$$

and using (1),

$$w(0) = -\frac{c}{r} + (R + \frac{c}{r})\int_0^\infty e^{-rs}f(s)\,ds. \tag{2}$$

The mean net present value decision rule adopted by the company can be stated as follows:

Start the project if $w(0) > 0$; do
not start the project if $w(0) \leq 0$.

The sign of $w(0)$ will depend on both the values of the constants c, r, and R and on the probability density function of the random completion time T.

Now suppose the project, having been supported for t years but not yet completed, is reevaluated to see if funding should be continued. Let $v_t(T)$ denote the net present value of the project *at the time t*, assuming it will be continued until completion. To compute $v_t(T)$ requires that we discount back to time t both the return R at completion time T and the costs being continuously expended over the interval from t to T. We obtain

$$v_t(T) = Re^{-r(T-t)} - \int_t^T ce^{-r(s-t)}ds$$

or, evaluating the integral,

$$v_t(T) = e^{-r(T-t)}(R + \frac{c}{r}) - \frac{c}{r}. \tag{3}$$

As before, we note that $v_t(T)$ is a random variable and so we define

$$w(t) = E[v_t(T)],$$

the mean net present value of the project at time t, *conditional on the event that $T > t$*, i.e., that the project has been operating from time 0 to t and will be continued until completed. Since $1 - F(t)$ is the probability that $T > t$, the density function of T conditional on $T > t$ has the value

$$\frac{f(s)}{1 - F(t)}$$

at any time $s > t$. Hence, using (3),

$$w(t) = -\frac{c}{r} + (R + \frac{c}{r})\int_t^\infty e^{-r(s-t)}\frac{f(s)}{1 - F(t)}\,ds$$

or, after simplifying the integral,

$$w(t) = -\frac{c}{r} + (R + \frac{c}{r})\frac{e^{rt}}{1 - F(t)} \int_t^\infty e^{-rs} f(s)\, ds. \tag{4}$$

Note that when $t = 0$ this formula reduces to that given for $w(0)$ in (2).

If $w(t) > 0$, then the company decides at time t to continue the project; if $w(t) \leq 0$, the project is better shut down at time t.

To illustrate these policy decisions, suppose first that T is exponentially distributed, i.e., $f(x) = be^{-bx}$ for $x \geq 0$ where b is a positive constant. (One can easily show that $E(T) = 1/b$ so b is the reciprocal of the mean completion time.) Now

$$\Pr(T > t) = 1 - F(t) = \int_t^\infty f(s)\, ds = e^{-bt}$$

and from (4),

$$\begin{aligned}
w(t) &= -\frac{c}{r} + (R + \frac{c}{r}) be^{(r+b)t} \int_t^\infty e^{-(r+b)s}\, ds \\
&= -\frac{c}{r} + (R + \frac{c}{r}) be^{(r+b)t} \frac{e^{-(r+b)t}}{(r+b)} \\
&= -\frac{c}{r} + \frac{b}{r+b}(R + \frac{c}{r}) \\
&= \frac{Rb - c}{r + b}.
\end{aligned}$$

Thus $w(t)$ is a constant independent of t and we conclude that if $w(0) > 0$ then $w(t) > 0$ for all t: a project once started is supported to completion by the company. Note also that in this special case the sign of $w(t)$ depends only on whether Rb is greater or less than c, and is not influenced by the discount rate r. (The quantity Rb is the project's average annual payoff until completion since it is the payoff R divided by $1/b$, the mean number of years until completion of the project. The quantity c is the corresponding annual cost.) These results, of course, depend on the assumed exponential density of the completion time T and are not generally true.

Suppose now that a project is worth starting, i.e., it has a positive mean net present value at $t = 0$. It is important to realize that such a project, if not completed by some subsequent time $t > 0$, can have a *negative* mean net present value at time t. If the project were reviewed at that time, we would conclude that it should be abandoned, even though it was worth starting when initially evaluated. What follows is a specific numerical example to illustrate this possibility.

Suppose the completion time T has probability density function f given by

$$f(x) = \begin{cases} 1/2 & \text{if } 0 \leq x \leq 1 \\ 1/2 & \text{if } 3 \leq x \leq 4 \\ 0 & \text{elsewhere.} \end{cases}$$

The project is as likely to be completed in the first year as the fourth year and if not completed in the first year is sure to require somewhere between two and three more years to complete. From (2) we compute

$$w(0) = -\frac{c}{r} + (R + \frac{c}{r})[\frac{1}{2}\int_0^1 e^{-rs}\,ds + \frac{1}{2}\int_3^4 e^{-rs}\,ds]$$

and evaluating the integrals and simplifying,

$$w(0) = -\frac{c}{r} + (R + \frac{c}{r})(1 - e^{-r} + e^{-3r} - e^{-4r})/2r.$$

Similarly, using (4) and noting that $1 - F(1) = P(T > 1) = 1/2$, we compute

$$w(1) = -\frac{c}{r} + (R + \frac{c}{r})2e^r \int_3^4 e^{-rs}\frac{1}{2}\,ds$$

from which

$$w(1) = -\frac{c}{r} + (R + \frac{c}{r})e^r(e^{-3r} - e^{-4r})/r.$$

If we put $c = 1$, $R = 2.5$, $r = .1$, and do the required calculations we find

$$w(0) = -10 + (12.5)(.828) > 0$$

but

$$w(1) = -10 + (12.5)(.779) < 0,$$

thus confirming that this project, once started and seen not to be completed by the end of the first year, is best terminated at that time. The return is large enough to make the first year's cost worth paying. But when that year proves to be too short to complete the project, the anticipated return is no longer sufficient to justify at least two more years of cash outlays.

4. Bibliographic Notes

Problem 1 is discussed and solved by Dean [3]. This solution exemplifies the sequential solution technique employed in *dynamic programming*, a subject with many important applications and a large literature. We list three general references whose bibliographies will lead the interested student to many other sources: Dreyfus and Law [4], Hillier and Lieberman [6], Wagner [13]. A short technical note by Boyd [2] shows how the ordinary process of long division can be formulated as a dynamic programming procedure. The volume by Howard [7] applies dynamic programming to Markovian decision processes. Techniques from dynamic programming are used by Marshall [11] to determine an optimal sequence of items or stimuli in testing the learning of a skill.

Problem 2, along with modified versions requiring more advanced methods of analysis, is solved by Lucas [10]. For a discussion of various measures of investment worth, only one of which (net present value) is used by Lucas, see Bierman and Smidt [1].

The general problem posed in Exercise 2 can be found in Mitten [12] and with variations in Dean [3] and Joyce [8]. A variation known as the "obstacle course problem" is discussed by Goodman [5]. All of these are special cases of the more general collection of "quiz show problems" introduced and solved by Kadane [9].

Exercises

1. A project requires the successful completion of three tasks in any order, but the project is terminated as soon as a task results in failure. The probability of success and the cost associated with each task are as follows:

Task Number	Probability of Success	Cost ($000's)
1	.8	5
2	.6	7
3	.7	8

Assume that the success or failure of each task is independent of the outcomes of the other tasks.

For each possible ordering of the three tasks, compute the mean project cost and thus verify that this project is carried out with least mean cost of $13,840 by trying its three tasks in the order 2, 1, 3. Using this optimal order, what is the probability that the project will be successfully completed?

2. To generalize Exercise 1, suppose now that there are n tasks with task number i having cost c_i and non-zero probability of success p_i. (The probability of failure is therefore $q_i = 1 - p_i$.) As before, all n independent tasks must be successfully completed, but the project concludes as soon as one task results in failure. Proceed as follows to prove the general result: *Minimum mean cost of the project occurs when tasks are attempted in the order of nondecreasing c_i/q_i ratios. Of course, tasks with zero cost should be tried first and tasks with zero failure rate should be tried last in any order among themselves.*

Step 1. Let the mean cost associated with an ordering of the tasks be denoted by $E(C;)$ with the ordering specified after the semicolon.

Investigate the effect of interchanging two neighboring tasks, say j and $j + 1$, by computing

$$E(C; 1, 2, \ldots, j, j + 1, \ldots, n) = c, \text{ say,}$$

and

$$E(C; 1, 2, \ldots, j + 1, j, \ldots, n) = c', \text{ say,}$$

and showing that

$$c' - c = p_1 p_2 \ldots p_{j-1}(c_{j+1} + p_{j+1} c_j - c_j - p_j c_{j+1}).$$

Step 2. Assuming no p_i equals 1 (equivalently, no q_i equals 0) and no cost c_i equals zero, show that

$$c' > c \quad \text{if and only if} \quad \frac{c_{j+1}}{q_{j+1}} > \frac{c_j}{q_j}.$$

Step 3. Complete the proof.

3. Consider the following special cases in Exercise 2. If all costs c_i are the same, then it makes sense to perform high-risk tasks first; if all probabilities of success p_i are the same, then it makes sense to perform low-cost tasks first. Verify that these intuitively reasonable conclusions follow from the general result in Exercise 2.

4. Apply the result of Exercise 2 to a project involving five tasks with costs and probabilities of success as follows:

Task Number	Probability of Success	Cost ($000's)
1	.2	16
2	.1	9
3	.3	12
4	.3	14
5	.1	10

Show that the least mean project cost of $10,176.40 occurs with either of two orderings of the tasks: 2, 5, 3, 1, 4 and 2, 5, 3, 4, 1.

5. Consider the foundation in Problem 1 of the text faced with two proposals with success probabilities and costs specified as follows:

$$p_1 = .7 \qquad p_2 = .3$$
$$c_1 = 50 \qquad c_2 = 20.$$

Show that the foundation maximizes its probability of achieving the project objective by adopting the following strategy: If the total amount budgeted for the project is B, then

if $0 \leq B < 20$, fund neither proposal;
if $20 \leq B < 50$, fund proposal 2 only;
if $50 \leq B < 70$, fund proposal 1 only;
if $70 \leq B$, fund both proposals.

Construct a table like Table 1 and a figure like Figure 1 for this example.

6. Consider Problem 1 of the text with

(a) three proposals: $p_1 = .7$ $p_2 = .3$ $p_3 = .4$
$c_1 = 5$ $c_2 = 2$ $c_3 = 6$

(b) four proposals: $p_1 = .7$ $p_2 = .3$ $p_3 = .5$ $p_4 = .4$
$c_1 = 5$ $c_2 = 2$ $c_3 = 6$ $c_4 = 3.$

In each case, determine $f_1(B)$, $f_2(B)$, ... for appropriate values of B and summarize your findings concerning the optimal allocation of funds to the competing proposals by means of a table like Table 1 and a figure like Figure 1. As in Figure 1, for each value of the total budget B, you should specify the alternatives to be funded and the total amount actually spent.

7. Write a computer program for determining the optimal solution of Problem 1 for arbitrary (but suitably limited) values of B, the total amount budgeted for the project, and n, the total number of independent alternatives seeking support. Your program, when applied to any particular problem, should require as input the values of B, n, p_i, c_i ($i = 1, 2, \ldots, n$), and should then generate as output the maximum probability $f_n(B)$ of achieving the research objective as well as the corresponding set of alternative proposals to be funded. If you can manage it, try to produce output in tabular form (as in Table 1) or in graphical form (as in Figure 1). Test your program on the illustrative example worked out in the text or on the examples in Exercise 6.

8. In Problem 2 of the text, suppose the random variable T is degenerate and is actually a constant ($= T_0$, say). Thus we are assuming that there is a known and fixed completion time for the project.

(a) Determine $v_0(T_0)$.

(b) Noting that $v_0(T_0)$ is now no longer a random variable, formulate the company's decision rule for accepting or rejecting the proposal.

(c) Assuming the project is undertaken at time 0, compute its value at time t for $0 < t < T_0$. Thus show that any project worth undertaking at $t = 0$ increases in value over time and therefore should be continued until completion.

9. In Problem 2 of the text, suppose the completion time T is uniformly distributed in (a,b), i.e., $f(x) = 1/(b - a)$ if $a \leq x \leq b$ and $f(x) = 0$ elsewhere.

(a) Determine $w(0)$ and $w(t)$ for all $t < b$.

(b) Suppose $w(0) > 0$ so the project is worth starting. If you reviewed the project at $t = a > 0$, then surely you would make the same decision since you knew at the outset that the project wouldn't be completed before elapsed time a. Prove this by showing that $w(0) > 0$ implies $w(a) > 0$.

(c) Show that $\lim_{t\to b} w(t) = R$. Explain why this is reasonable.

(d) Show that a project worth starting is worth being continued to completion, i.e., if $w(0) > 0$, then $w(t) > 0$ for all t in (a,b). Explain why this is intuitively reasonable.

10. In Problem 2 of the text, suppose the completion time T is a random variable with a two-parameter exponential probability density, i.e.,

$$f(x) = \begin{cases} be^{-b(x-a)} & \text{if } x \geq a \\ 0 & \text{if } x < a, \end{cases}$$

where a and b are positive constants. This means that T is sure to be at least a, but beyond that it is exponential with parameter b. (One can easily verify that $E(T) = a + 1/b$.)

(a) Determine $w(t)$ for $0 \leq t < a$ and for $t \geq a$ and sketch a graph of $w(t)$ for $t \geq 0$.

(b) Show that $w(0) > 0$ implies $w(t) > 0$ for all t so that such a project, once started, is carried out to completion.

11. In Problem 2 of the text, suppose the completion time T is Gamma distributed, i.e., $f(x) = k(a,b)\,x^{a-1}e^{-bx}$ for $x > 0$, where $a \geq 1$ and $b > 0$ are constants. $k(a,b)$ is determined by the requirement that f be a probability density function, that is, $\int_0^\infty f(x)\,dx = 1$. (It turns out that $k(a,b) = b^a/\Gamma(a)$ where the Gamma function is defined by $\Gamma(a) = \int_0^\infty y^{a-1}e^{-y}\,dy$.)

Show that $w(t)$ is no longer a constant independent of t (as in the case of an exponentially distributed completion time worked out in the text), but nevertheless, if $w(0) > 0$ then $w(t) > 0$. Thus a project, once started, is worthy of continued support until completion. (Note. This generalizes the result of the text since the exponential distribution is the special case of the Gamma distribution when the parameter $a = 1$.)

12. The special case of Problem 2 with completion time T having probability density function f given by

$$f(x) = \begin{cases} 1/2 & \text{if } 0 \leq x \leq 1 \\ .1/2 & \text{if } 3 \leq x \leq 4 \\ 0 & \text{elsewhere,} \end{cases}$$

was considered in the text. It was shown that this project (with $c = 1$, $R = 2.5$, $r = .1$) had $w(0) > 0$ but $w(1) < 0$. Such a project, if not completed by $t = 1$, should be terminated at that time.

Suppose now that this project, started at $t = 0$, is reviewed at time t $(0 < t < 1)$. Sketch a graph of $w(t)$ for $0 \leq t \leq 1$ and show that the smallest elapsed time after which the review leads to the project's termination is (to two decimal place accuracy) $t^* = .82$ years. Thus a review before t^* keeps the project alive, but a review after t^* kills it.

13. Construct another example (different from that in the text) to illustrate that a project worthy of being started at $t = 0$ can become unattractive if not completed by some later time t and therefore would be terminated if reviewed at time t.

Bibliography

1. Bierman, H. and S. Smidt, *The Capital Budgeting Decision*, New York: Macmillan, 1960.
2. Boyd, D. W., "Long Division: An Example of Dynamic Programming," *AIEE Transactions*, vol. 6 (1974), 365–366.
3. Dean, B. V., "Stochastic Networks in Research Planning," pp.235–266, in Yovits, M. C. *et al* (Eds.), *Research Planning Effectiveness*, New York: Gordon & Breach, 1966.
4. Dreyfus, S. E. and A. M. Law, *The Art and Theory of Dynamic Programming*, New York: Academic Press, 1977.
5. Goodman, L., "On Optimal Arrangements in Some Learning Situations," *Bulletin Mathematical Biophysics*, vol. 14 (1952), 307–312.
6. Hillier, F. S. and G. J. Lieberman, *Introduction to Operations Research*, third edition, San Francisco: Holden-Day, 1980.
7. Howard, R. A., *Dynamic Probabilistic Systems*, vol. 1: *Markovian Models*, New York: Wiley, 1971.
8. Joyce, W. B., "Organization of Unsuccessful R & D Projects," *IEEE Transactions on Engineering Management*, vol. EM-18 (1971), 57–65.
9. Kadane, J. B., "Quiz Show Problems," *Journal of Mathematical Analysis and Applications*, vol. 26 (1969), 609–623.
10. Lucas, R. E., "Optimal Management of a Research and Development Project," *Management Science*, vol. 17 (1971), 679–697.
11. Marshall, S. P., "Sequential Item Selection: Optimal and Heuristic Policies," *Journal of Mathematical Psychology*, vol. 23 (1981), 134–152.
12. Mitten, L. G., "An Analytic Solution to the Least Cost Testing Sequence Problem," *Journal of Industrial Engineering*, vol. 11 (1960), 17.
13. Wagner, H. M., *Principles of Operations Research*, second edition, Englewood Cliffs: Prentice-Hall, 1975, especially Chapters 8 and 10.

Chapter 4
Stochastic Learning Models

1. Introduction

How subjects learn has long been of interest to psychologists. Large amounts of data are available from experiments in which various outputs (responses) of subjects have been studied as functions of a range of experimenter-controlled input factors (stimuli). To account for these input-output relationships is a task for the theorist. In this unit we first consider a mathematical model for learning (the so-called all-or-none or one-element model) as applied by Bower [7] to a paired-associate experiment. After characterizing the formal structure of this model, we introduce a slight generalization, the two-stage all-or-none model. The analysis of a learning experiment using stimulus sampling theory and leading to a three-state Markov chain is outlined in some detail in the Exercises. These models are samples from a wide variety of stochastic learning models, mainly developed since 1950, and applicable to many different experimental situations. A guide for further reading in mathematical learning theory concludes the unit.

2. The Experiment and the Model

In Bower's experiment, 29 subjects learned to associate the correct integer, either 1 or 2, with each of ten different pairs of consonant letters. For five of the pairs, the integer 1 was the correct response, for the other five the integer 2 was correct. A subject was shown one of the consonant pairs, the subject responded with 1 or 2, and the correct response was then given by the experimenter. After a short time interval, a second consonant pair was presented and the procedure repeated until each of the ten pairs had been presented once, completing one trial of the experiment for that subject. The deck of ten cards containing the consonant pairs (the stimuli) was shuffled before each trial and the experiment continued until the subject made two consecutive errorless passes through the deck.

For each subject and each stimulus, the experiment produces a sequence of responses (each response being correct or incorrect) over successive trials. The experimenter can then compute such statistical features of the data as the total number of errors per subject-stimulus sequence, the average frequency of errors on each trial, the average trial number of the last error,

49

etc. A theoretical model is then tested by how well it predicts or fits such observed statistical features of the data.

In the mathematical model, the stimulus is represented by a single undefined entity, a construct called a *stimulus element*. The following assumptions are made:

1. The stimulus element is in one of two *states* on each trial, either state C (*conditioned* to the correct response) or state C' (*not conditioned*).
2. The stimulus element is in state C' at the beginning of the experiment, i.e., at the start of trial number 1.
3. Each time a particular stimulus is presented, the subject samples (or inspects) the corresponding stimulus element. If it is in state C, then the subject is sure to make the correct response. If, however, the stimulus element is found in its unconditioned state C', then the subject has only a lesser probability, say $g < 1$, of responding correctly. (g is a guessing parameter. So in Bower's experiment, where the response is either 1 or 2, g was put equal to $1/2$ to represent the subject's chance of merely guessing the correct response.)
4. Finally, the model must specify the effect of a reinforcement (i.e., the subject's hearing or seeing the correct response on each trial) on the state of the stimulus element. On each trial, if the stimulus element is already in state C, it stays there. But if it is in state C', then it undergoes a transition to state C with probability c $(0 < c < 1)$.

Assumption 3 embodies the all-or-none feature of the model: when the stimulus is presented, the corresponding response is either known perfectly or known not at all so that merely a guess at the correct response is made. The model is extraordinarily simple and generalizations immediately suggest themselves. More than one stimulus element may reasonably be assumed to correspond to each stimulus. On each trial, the subject may sample more than just one stimulus element and the subject's response might then depend on how many and which of the stimulus elements are conditioned to the correct response. Such more elaborate models have been studied and we shall say more about them further on, but now let us return to the simple one-element all-or-none model.

3.   Consequences of the Model

It is convenient to introduce a random variable X_n that indicates the nature of the response (for a given subject and stimulus) on trial n:

$$X_n = \begin{cases} 0 & \text{if a correct response is given on trial } n \\ 1 & \text{if an error occurs on trial } n. \end{cases}$$

(Such a counting random variable appears quite often in probability theory and its applications. It takes a qualitative outcome of an experimental trial (correct response or incorrect response, for example) and maps it into the numerical value 0 or 1.)

Let C_n and C'_n denote the stimulus element being in state C or C', respectively, at the end of trial n. We now derive some consequences of the assumptions made in the model and then see how they fit the experimental data.

Result 1. The probability of an error diminishes as the experiment proceeds and approaches zero according to the formula

$$\Pr(X_n = 1) = (1 - c)^{n-1}(1 - g) \qquad n = 1, 2, \ldots . \tag{1}$$

Proof. Errors can occur only when the stimulus element is unconditioned, and they occur then with probability $1 - g$. Hence

$$\Pr(X_n = 1) = \Pr(C'_{n-1})(1 - g).$$

But C'_{n-1} occurs if and only if the stimulus element, known to start in state C' at the beginning of trial 1 (Assumption 2) stays in this state at the end of trials $1, 2, \ldots, n - 1$. For, by Assumption 4, were it ever to leave this state and move to C, then it would stay there. Since the probability of staying in C' on any trial is $(1 - c)$, we have $\Pr(C'_{n-1}) = (1 - c)^{n-1}$ and thus Formula (1).

Since $0 < c < 1$ and $1 - g > 0$, this probability decreases steadily and approaches zero as $n \to \infty$, as claimed.

Result 2. Let T denote the total number of errors made by a subject on a given stimulus. Then the mean (expected value) of T is given by

$$E(T) = \frac{1 - g}{c}. \tag{2}$$

Proof. Note first that T is given by the sum $X_1 + X_2 + \cdots$ since each X_n contributes 1 to the sum if the n-*th* trial produces an error and contributes 0 to the sum otherwise. Hence

$$E(T) = E(\sum_{n=1}^{\infty} X_n)$$

$$= \sum_{n=1}^{\infty} [E(X_n)].$$

But

$$E(X_n) = 1 \cdot \Pr(X_n = 1) + 0 \cdot \Pr(X_n = 0)$$
$$= (1 - c)^{n-1}(1 - g), \text{ from (1)}.$$

Hence

$$E(T) = (1 - g) \sum_{n=1}^{\infty} (1 - c)^{n-1}$$

and summing the geometric series we obtain (2).

Note that we are able to find the mean value of random variable T without first knowing its probability distribution. The next result derives this distribution.

Result 3.

$$\Pr(T = n) = \begin{cases} bg & \text{if } n = 0 \\ b(1 - b)^n/(1 - c) & \text{if } n \geq 1 \end{cases} \tag{3}$$

where

$$b = \frac{c}{1 - g(1 - c)}. \tag{4}$$

Proof. Once the subject learns (i.e., the stimulus element enters state C), no errors can be made. But the subject, in theory at least, can keep *guessing* correctly even if learning hasn't yet taken place (i.e., the stimulus element is in state C'). Thus the event $T = 0$ can occur in the following mutually exclusive ways: the subject responds correctly on trials $1, 2, \ldots, k$ by guessing, but actually *first* learns on trial k, for $k = 1, 2, \ldots$. The probability of correct guessing on trials 1 to k is g^k and the probability of first learning on trial k is given by

$$\Pr(C_1' C_2' \ldots C_{k-1}' C_k) = (1 - c)^{k-1} c.$$

Hence

$$\Pr(T = 0) = \sum_{k=1}^{\infty} g^k (1 - c)^{k-1} c$$

$$= gc \sum_{k=1}^{\infty} [g(1 - c)]^{k-1}$$

$$= gc \frac{1}{1 - g(1 - c)} = gb,$$

as claimed in (3).

If $n \geq 1$, the event $T = n$ can occur in the following mutually exclusive ways: the subject *first* learns on trial $n + k$ and among the guesses made on trials $1, 2, \ldots, n + k$, there are exactly n incorrect and k correct responses, for $k = 0, 1, \ldots$. The probability of first learning on trial $n + k$ is given by

$$\Pr(C_1' C_2' \ldots C_{n+k-1}' C_{n+k}) = (1 - c)^{n+k-1} c.$$

Since the $n + k$ guessing trials are independent and the probability of an incorrect guess is $1 - g$ on each such trial, the probability of exactly n incorrect responses is obtained from the binomial distribution. Thus

$$\Pr(T = n) = \sum_{k=0}^{\infty} (1 - c)^{n+k-1} c \binom{n + k}{n} (1 - g)^n g^k.$$

Rewriting, we have

$$\Pr(T = n) = (1 - c)^{n-1} c (1 - g)^n \sum_{k=0}^{\infty} \binom{n + k}{n} [g(1 - c)]^k. \qquad (5)$$

But

$$\binom{n + k}{n} = \frac{(n + k)(n + k - 1) \dots (n + 1)}{k!}$$

and writing the numerator with factors in reverse order,

$$\binom{n + k}{n} = \frac{(n + 1)(n + 2) \dots (n + k)}{k!}.$$

Now let $a = -n - 1$ and note that

$$\binom{n + k}{n} = (-1)^k \frac{a(a - 1) \dots (a - k + 1)}{k!}.$$

Hence we recognize the sum in (5) as the binomial series expansion* (convergent since $0 < g(1 - c) < 1$)

$$\sum_{k=0}^{\infty} (-1)^k \frac{a(a - 1) \dots (a - k + 1)}{k!} [g(1 - c)]^k = [1 - g(1 - c)]^a.$$

Thus

$$\Pr(T = n) = (1 - c)^{n-1} c (1 - g)^n [1 - g(1 - c)]^{-n-1}$$

$$= \frac{c}{1 - g(1 - c)} \left[\frac{(1 - g)(1 - c)}{1 - g(1 - c)} \right]^n \frac{1}{1 - c}$$

$$= \frac{b(1 - b)^n}{1 - c},$$

and the proof of (3) is complete.

Many additional results can be derived in a similar fashion. (See Bower [7] for further details.) But let us briefly illustrate how the results derived are compared to observed experimental statistics.

Consider, for example, equation (1) for the probability of an error on trial number n. In Bower's experiment, guessing is done between just two possible responses (1 or 2) and so g is taken to be $1/2$. But a value for the parameter c of the model is also needed. Although many difficult problems in statistical estimation arise in applying learning models to data, in this case it seems quite reasonable to estimate c by equating an experimentally obtained average number of errors to the theoretically predicted mean given

*For a discussion of the binomial series, see the chapter on infinite series in almost any calculus book.

in equation (2). Bower found in his experiment that the average number of errors per item was 1.45. Equating $E(T)$ in (2) to 1.45, the estimated value of c turns out to be .345 (Bower uses .344). Hence, from (1), Bower obtained $(.5)(.656)^{n-1}$ as the theoretically predicted proportion of errors on trial n for $n = 1, 2, \ldots$. The corresponding observed proportions can be calculated from the experimental data. The excellent agreement between observed and theoretically predicted curves (so-called *learning curves*) is shown in Figure 1.

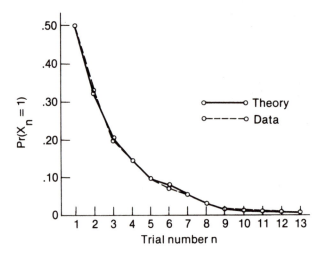

Figure 1. $\Pr(X_n = 1)$, the probability of an incorrect response over successive trials of the experiment; from Bower [7, p.260].

With c estimated, (3) and (4) yield theoretically predicted values for the distribution of T, the total number of errors per stimulus-response pair and for a given subject. Again (see Figure 2) there is substantial agreement between theory and observation.

4. Extensions and Further Reading

The all-or-none model, first introduced by Estes [13] as a part of his general development of stimulus sampling theory, accounts for data quite well in simple experiments. Although still used (see Brainerd and Howe [8], for example) it proves inadequate for more complex learning situations. (See Suppes and Ginsberg [35].) Some idea of the direction of generalization suggested in the literature can be better understood if the formal structure of the all-or-none model is made clear first.

A collection $\{C, C'\}$ of two states is postulated, exactly one of which a subject occupies on each trial. There is introduced a stochastic mechanism

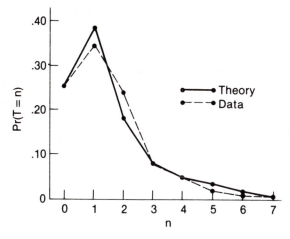

Figure 2. Distribution of T, the total number of errors per stimulus-response pair; from Bower [7, p.261].

governing state to state transitions, summarized by the transition probability matrix

$$P = \begin{array}{c} \\ C \\ C' \end{array} \begin{array}{cc} C & C' \\ \begin{pmatrix} 1 & 0 \\ c & 1-c \end{pmatrix} \end{array}, \tag{6}$$

recognized as a transition matrix of a Markov chain. The learning states C and C' have error probabilities associated with them given by the column vector

$$\begin{pmatrix} 0 \\ g' \end{pmatrix} \qquad (g' = 1 - g)$$

which merely symbolizes the fact that in state C there is a zero probability and in state C' a probability equal to g' of making a response error. Finally there is the initial state row vector $(0,1)$ which expresses the assumption that we are certain to start in the unconditioned state.

This Markov model has one additional noteworthy feature. We saw in (1) that the error probability goes to zero with n. This is reflected in the transition probability matrix governing transitions from the initial time to trial n. Since this n-step transition matrix is just the n-th power of the matrix for 1-step (trial) transitions, it is easy to establish (Exercise 8) that

$$P^n = \begin{pmatrix} 1 & 0 \\ 1 - (1-c)^n & (1-c)^n \end{pmatrix}. \tag{7}$$

It is then clear that the probability of a transition from state C' to state C approaches 1 as $n \to \infty$ and once in C, one stays there. That is, state C is a so-called *absorbing state*.

If the learning situation is more complex than suitable for this one-stage all-or-none structure, a natural generalization is to assume that two or more learning stages are involved in mastery of the task. The simplest two-stage all-or-none model would postulate three possible states: C', an initial unlearned guessing state with probability g' of an error; I, an intermediate (stage 1 but not stage 2) state with some lower error probability e; and a learned state C, with a zero error probability. Thus corresponding to the state set, the transition probability matrix P, the error probability vector, and the initial state probability vector for the all-or-none Markov model, we now have state set $\{C, I, C'\}$, a transition matrix of the form

$$
P = \begin{array}{c} \\ C \\ I \\ C' \end{array}
\begin{array}{ccc}
C & I & C' \\
\end{array}
\left(
\begin{array}{ccc}
1 & 0 & 0 \\
b & 1-b & 0 \\
0 & a & 1-a
\end{array}
\right)
$$

where a and b are model parameters (corresponding to the single parameter c in the matrix for the one-stage model), an error probability vector

$$
\begin{pmatrix} 0 \\ e \\ g' \end{pmatrix},
$$

and an initial state probability vector $(0, 0, 1)$.

And one can have variations within this two-stage Markov model (different forms for the transition matrix, for example) as well as higher-order models. Such models are developed by Atkinson and Crothers [2], Bernbach [4], Friedman, Trabasso, and Mosberg [14], Greeno [15], Kintsch and Morris [21], and Theios [36] for experiments involving forgetting, free recall and recognition, and avoidance learning. All these theorists motivated their two-stage theory from psychological considerations, ran experiments that provided data from which parameters of the model could be estimated, and predicted various learning process statistics that could be compared (and which gave close fits) to their observed counterparts.

Naturally, the more complex the Markov model the more difficult is the derivation of the formulas from which predictions can be made. The matrix theory developed by Kemeny and Snell [20] is applied to a particular learning model in their book. Bernbach [5] and Millward [27] show how to use the theory of Markov chains to develop learning process statistics for general Markov learning models. Computer programs can be written to generate predictions for any particular model and set of parameters. In fact, Bernbach shows how his very general formulas can be used to get various learning process statistics, including error probabilities, total number of errors, etc., for Bower's all-or-none model considered earlier in this unit.

There is a very large literature devoted to mathematical learning theory. There are books by Atkinson, Bower, and Crothers [1], Bush and

Mosteller [9], Kintsch [22], Levine and Burke [24], Niemark and Estes [29], and Norman [30]. The valuable review articles by Atkinson and Estes [3], Greeno and Bjork [17], and Sternberg [34] contain extensive bibliographies. Mathematical models of learning get some attention in the book by Murdock [28] and the review article of Cotton [11]. And there are textbooks on mathematical psychology (Coombs, Dawes, and Tversky [10] with an associated workbook [6], Greeno [16], Laming [23], Restle and Greeno [31]) that have chapters on learning theory.

Finally, we mention for the interested reader a number of references (Crothers [12], Groen and Atkinson [18], Karush and Dear [19], Smallwood [32,33]) in which all-or-none and more general learning models are used in an analysis of stimulus presentation sequences. These authors have computer-assisted instruction in mind and are interested in developing presentation strategies that optimize learning efficiency or other learning-related objectives. Marshall [26] combines techniques from dynamic programming and probability to investigate the effect of ordering of items or stimuli in testing the learning of a skill.

Exercises

1. In Bower's model, the random variable $T = \sum_{n=1}^{\infty} X_n$ is the total number of errors made by a subject. Give interpretations for the variables L, $R_{j,n}$, R_j, and R, defined as follows:

(a) $L = j$ if $X_j = 1$ and $X_k = 0$ for $k > j$.

(b) $R_{j,n} = \begin{cases} 1 & \text{if } X_k = 1 \text{ for } k = n, n+1, \ldots, n+j-1, \\ 0 & \text{otherwise.} \end{cases}$

(c) $R_j = \sum_{n=1}^{\infty} R_{j,n}$.

(d) $R = \sum_{j=1}^{\infty} R_j$. (Distinguish between the runs counted by R and by $R_1 - R_2$.)

2. With notation as in Exercise 1, (a) show that $T = R_1$ and (b) verify that for the response sequence $1,1,1,0,0,1,1,0,0,0,0,0,\ldots$ we have $L = 7$, $R_1 = 5$, $R_2 = 3$, $R_3 = 1$, and hence $R = 9$.

3. Suppose an error occurring on trial number n is weighted by the factor w_n and define $Y_n = w_n X_n$. Let $S = \sum_{n=1}^{\infty} Y_n$. (Note that S reduces to T, the total number of errors made by the subject, if $w_n = 1$ for all n.) Show that

(a) $E(S) = (1 - g)/c^2$ if $w_n = n$.

(b) $E(S) = ((1 - g)/(1 - c)) \log(1/c)$ if $w_n = 1/n$.

4. Let Z denote the number of the trial on which the last error occurs. Show that

(a) $\Pr(Z = n) = \begin{cases} bg & \text{if } n = 0 \\ b(1 - g)(1 - c)^{n-1} & \text{if } n = 1, 2, 3, \ldots. \end{cases}$

(b) $E(Z) = b(1 - g)/c^2$.

5. For positive integers n and k, show that

(a) $\Pr(X_{n+k} = 1 \mid X_n = 1) = (1 - c)^k(1 - g)$.

(b) $\Pr(X_n = 1, X_{n+k} = 1) = (1 - c)^{n+k-1}(1 - g)^2$.

6. With notation as in Exercise 1, show that the expected number of error runs is given by

$$E(R_1 - R_2) = (1 - g)(g + c - gc)/c.$$

Hint. In computing $E(R_2)$, note that $E(R_{2,n}) = E(X_n X_{n+1})$ and use the result of Exercise 5(b).

7. Let T denote the total number of errors made by the subject. Show that

$$\mathrm{Var}(T) = \frac{1 - g}{c} + (1 - 2c)\left(\frac{1 - g}{c}\right)^2.$$

Hint. Recall that $\mathrm{Var}(T) = E(T^2) - [E(T)]^2$. In computing $E(T^2)$, note that $E(X_n X_{n+k}) = \Pr(X_n = 1, X_{n+k} = 1)$ and use the result of Exercise 5(b).

8. The 1-step transition probability matrix (6) can be written in the form

$$P = \begin{pmatrix} p^{(1)}(C|C) & p^{(1)}(C'|C) \\ p^{(1)}(C|C') & p^{(1)}(C'|C') \end{pmatrix} = \begin{pmatrix} 1 & 0 \\ c & 1-c \end{pmatrix}$$

where, for example, $p^{(1)}(C|C') = c$ denotes the probability of ending up in state C after 1 trial, given that the subject started in state C'. Similarly, define the n-step transition probability matrix $p^{(n)}$ as follows for $n = 1, 2, \ldots$:

$$P^{(n)} = \begin{pmatrix} p^{(n)}(C|C) & p^{(n)}(C'|C) \\ p^{(n)}(C|C') & p^{(n)}(C'|C') \end{pmatrix}$$

where now, for example, $p^{(n)}(C|C')$ denotes the probability of ending up in state C after n trials, given that the subject started in state C'.

(a) Show that $P^{(2)} = P \cdot P = P^2 = \begin{pmatrix} 1 & 0 \\ c(2 - c) & (1 - c)^2 \end{pmatrix}$.

(b) More generally, show for any positive integer n that $P^{(n)} = P^n$, thus verifying that the n-step transition probability matrix is the n-th power of the 1-step transition probability matrix.

(c) Prove that P^n is given by the matrix in (7).

Exercises 9–13 consider a simplified version of *stimulus sampling theory* (see Atkinson and Estes [3], Kintsch [22, Chapter 3]), which we summarize here. Think of a learning experiment in which a subject is seated before a box with two lights and is asked to predict on each trial whether the red or the green light will come on. After his response (A_1:red, A_2:green), one of the lights comes on (E_1:red, E_2:green), thus informing him whether his prediction was correct or incorrect. (To say that response A_i is reinforced means that reinforcing event E_i occurs.) The experimenter controls the choice of E_1 or E_2 by adopting a *reinforcement schedule* as specified in Table 1. Each entry in the table is the probability with which the experimenter makes her choice (E_1 or E_2) following observation of the subject's prediction (A_1 or A_2).

		Experimenter's Choice	
		E_1	E_2
Subject's	A_1	$1 - a$	a
Prediction	A_2	b	$1 - b$

Table 1. Experimenter's Reinforcement Schedule.

We first consider the special case $a = 0.5$, $b = 1$. This reinforcement schedule means that if the subject chooses A_1, then he is rewarded (reinforced) with probability 0.5, i.e., he has a 50-50 chance of being told he made the correct prediction. But if the subject chooses A_2, then he is certain to be told he made the wrong prediction and so is sure not to be rewarded.

The task is to determine the subject's behavior after a large number of such trials. Does he ultimately learn always to make response A_1?

In the stimulus sampling model, one imagines the existence of two constructs, so-called *stimulus elements* labeled S_1 and S_2. Each stimulus element is conditioned to exactly one response (either A_1 or A_2) at the start of each trial. The subject decides which response to make on each trial by first choosing at random one of the two stimulus elements. (S_1 and S_2 therefore each have probability $1/2$ of being chosen.) He then makes that response identified as the one to which the selected stimulus element is conditioned.

The experimenter then contributes E_1 or E_2 according to the specifications of the reinforcement schedule. The selected stimulus element is either already conditioned to the reinforced response or it is not. If it is, then it stays so for the next trial. If it is not, then it becomes conditioned to the reinforced response with probability c ($0 < c < 1$) and therefore remains conditioned to the other response with probability $1 - c$.

A stimulus element not sampled (chosen) on a trial does not change its state of conditioning on that trial. And the probability c stays fixed and

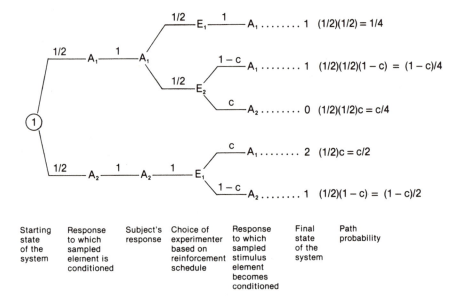

Starting state of the system	Response to which sampled element is conditioned	Subject's response	Choice of experimenter based on reinforcement schedule	Response to which sampled stimulus element becomes conditioned	Final state of the system	Path probability

Figure 3. Tree diagram for transitions starting in state 1.

is unaffected by the trial number or by the events occurring on preceding trials.

Since a stimulus element is conditioned to either response A_1 or A_2, the number of elements in each conditioning state is known if we know how many are conditioned to response A_1. The state of the system is therefore defined as the number of stimulus elements conditioned to A_1. Thus the system can be in one of three states at any trial: state 0, state 1, or state 2.

Exercises 9–13 complete the analysis of this Markov chain learning model.

9. Use the rules of stimulus sampling theory to derive the following transition probability matrix:

$$P = \begin{array}{c} \\ 0 \\ 1 \\ 2 \end{array} \begin{pmatrix} \begin{array}{ccc} 0 & 1 & 2 \end{array} \\ \begin{array}{ccc} 1-c & c & 0 \\ c/4 & 1-3c/4 & c/2 \\ 0 & c/2 & 1-c/2 \end{array} \end{pmatrix}$$

Hint. The tree diagram in Figure 3 illustrates the computation of the transition probabilities in the second row, i.e., assuming the system starts in state 1. A similar analysis, starting with the system in state 0 and state 2, produces the first and third rows of matrix P.

10. Check that P is a *regular* matrix, i.e., that there exists some positive integer k such that the matrix P^k has all positive entries.

11. From the theory of finite Markov chains (see Kemeny and Snell [20]), it follows that the regular transition probability matrix P has a unique fixed-point probability vector $\mathbf{w}$. If $\mathbf{w} = (w_0\ w_1\ w_2)$, then

$$w_0 + w_1 + w_2 = 1 \tag{8}$$

and w_i is interpreted as the long-run steady state probability of finding the system in state i. The theory tells us that these probabilities are independent of the starting state of the system and can be determined by solving the vector equation

$$\mathbf{w} = \mathbf{w}P$$

(which is a system of three simultaneous linear equations for the unknowns w_0, w_1, and w_2) together with condition (8). Do this and thus show that $\mathbf{w} = (1/9\ \ 4/9\ \ 4/9)$.

12. The subject makes response A_1 with probability 0 if the system is in state 0, with probability $1/2$ if the system is in state 1, and with probability 1 if the system is in state 2. Using the steady-state probabilities calculated in Exercise 11, show that the limiting steady-state probability that the subject makes response A_1 is $2/3$. Thus our stimulus sampling theory predicts that the subject will ultimately settle down to responding A_1 in about 2 out of each 3 trials.

13. Keep all the assumptions of the stimulus sampling theory, but now assume the experimenter adopts the so-called "non-contingent" reinforcement schedule given by $a = 1 - k$, $b = k$ with $0 < k < 1$. This means that the experimenter chooses E_1 with probability k and E_2 with probability $1 - k$ no matter what the subject does. Show that

(a) the transition probability matrix is now given by

$$P = \begin{array}{c} 0 \\ 1 \\ 2 \end{array} \begin{pmatrix} 1 - kc & kc & 0 \\ (1-k)c/2 & 1 - c/2 & kc/2 \\ 0 & (1-k)c & 1 - (1-k)c \end{pmatrix}.$$

with column headings $0 \quad 1 \quad 2$

(b) the matrix P is regular.

(c) the fixed-point probability vector is given by

$$\mathbf{w} = ((1-k)^2\ \ 2k(1-k)\ \ k^2).$$

(d) the limiting probability with which the subject makes response A_1 equals k.

Bibliography

1. Atkinson, R. C., G. H. Bower, and E. J. Crothers, *An Introduction to Mathematical Learning Theory*, New York: Wiley, 1965.

2. Atkinson, R. C. and E. J. Crothers, "A Comparison of Paired-Associate Learning Models Having Different Acquisition and Retention Axioms," *Journal of Mathematical Psychology*, vol. 1 (1964), 285–315.

3. Atkinson, R. C. and W. K. Estes, "Stimulus Sampling Theory," Chapter 10, pp.121–268 in [25].

4. Bernbach, H. A., "A Forgetting Model for Paired-Associate Learning," *Journal of Mathematical Psychology*, vol. 2 (1965), 128–144.

5. Bernbach, H. A., "Derivation of Learning Process Statistics for a General Markov Model," *Psychometrika*, vol. 31 (1966), 225–234.

6. Blair, W. C., M. F. O'Connor, and A. W. Pollatsek, *Workbook for Mathematical Psychology, an Elementary Introduction*, Englewood Cliffs: Prentice-Hall, 1970.

7. Bower, G. H., "Application of a Model to Paired-Associate Learning," *Psychometrika*, vol. 26 (1961), 255–280.

8. Brainerd, C. J. and M. L. Howe, "Developmental Invariance in a Mathematical Model of Associative Learning," *Child Development*, vol. 51 (1980), 349–363.

9. Bush, R. R. and F. Mosteller, *Stochastic Models for Learning*, New York: Wiley, 1955.

10. Coombs, C. H., R. M. Dawes, and A. Tversky, *Mathematical Psychology, An Elementary Introduction*, Englewood Cliffs: Prentice-Hall, 1970.

11. Cotton, J. W., "Models of Learning," *Annual Review of Psychology*, vol. 27 (1976), 155–187.

12. Crothers, E. J.,, "Learning Model Solution to a Problem in Constrained Optimization," *Journal of Mathematical Psychology*, vol. 2 (1965), 19–25.

13. Estes, W. K., "Learning Theory and the New Mental Chemistry," *Psychological Review*, vol. 67 (1960), 207–223.

14. Friedman, M. P., T. Trabasso, and L. Mosberg, "Tests of a Mixed Model for Paired-Associate Learning with Overlapping Stimuli," *Journal of Mathematical Psychology*, vol. 4 (1967), 316–334.

15. Greeno, J. G., "Paired-Associate Learning with Short-Term Retention: Mathematical Analysis and Data Regarding Identification of Parameters," *Journal of Mathematical Psychology*, vol. 4 (1967), 430–472.

16. Greeno, J. G., *Elementary Theoretical Psychology*, Reading, Mass.: Addison-Wesley, 1968.

17. Greeno, J. G. and R. A. Bjork, "Mathematical Learning Theory and the New 'Mental Forestry'," pp. 81–116 in Mussen, P. H. and M. R. Rosenzweig (Eds.), *Annual Review of Psychology*, vol. 24, Palo Alto: Annual Reviews, 1973.

18. Groen, G. J. and R. C. Atkinson, "Models for Optimizing the Learning Process," *Psychological Bulletin*, vol. 66 (1966), 309–320.

19. Karush, W. and R. E. Dear, "Optimal Stimulus Presentation Strategy for a Stimulus Sampling Model of Learning," *Journal of Mathematical Psychology*, vol. 3 (1966), 19–47.

20. Kemeny, J. G. and J. L. Snell, *Finite Markov Chains*, Princeton: Van Nostrand, 1959.

21. Kintsch, W. and C. J. Morris, "Application of a Markov Model to Free Recall and Recognition," *Journal of Experimental Psychology*, vol. 69 (1965), 200–206.

22. Kintsch, W., *Learning, Memory, and Conceptual Processes*, New York: Wiley, 1970.

23. Laming, D., *Mathematical Psychology*, New York: Academic Press, 1973.

24. Levine, G. and C. J. Burke, *Mathematical Model Techniques for Learning Theories*, New York: Academic Press, 1972.

25. Luce, R. D., R. R. Bush, and E. Galanter (Eds.) *Handbook of Mathematical Psychology*, vol. 2, New York: Wiley, 1963.

26. Marshall, S. P., "Sequential Item Selection: Optimal and Heuristic Policies," *Journal of Mathematical Psychology*, vol. 23 (1981), 134–152.

27. Millward, R. B., "Derivations of Learning Statistics from Absorbing Markov Chains," *Psychometrika*, vol. 34 (1969), 215–232.

28. Murdock, B. B. Jr., *Human Memory: Theory and Data*, Potomac, Md.: Erlbaum, 1974.

29. Niemark, E. D. and W. K. Estes (Eds.), *Stimulus Sampling Theory*, San Francisco: Holden-Day, 1967.

30. Norman, M. F., *Markov Processes and Learning Models*, New York: Academic Press, 1972.

31. Restle, F. and J. G. Greeno, *Introduction to Mathematical Psychology*, Reading: Addison-Wesley, 1970.

32. Smallwood, R. D., *A Decision Structure for Teaching Machines*, Cambridge: M.I.T. Press, 1962.

33. Smallwood, R. D., "The Analysis of Economic Teaching Strategies for a Simple Learning Model," *Journal of Mathematical Psychology*, vol. 8 (1971), 285–301.

34. Sternberg, S., "Stochastic Learning Theory," Chapter 9, pp.1–120 in [25].

35. Suppes, P. and R. Ginsberg, "A Fundamental Property of All-Or-None Models, Binomial Distribution of Responses Prior to Conditioning, with Application to Concept Formation in Children," *Psychological Review*, vol. 70 (1963), 139–161.

36. Theios, J., "Simple Conditioning as Two-Stage All-Or-None Learning," *Psychological Review*, vol. 70 (1963), 403–417.

Chapter 5
Glottochronology

1. Introduction

All languages change as time goes by. Dramatic evidence is given by Hockett [11, p.365] who presents nine passages, all in English, but originally written about a hundred years apart. The most current is a 1749 passage from *The History of Tom Jones*, the earliest from the Blickling Homily dated 971. His conclusion is clear: "a millenium of phylogenetic change has sufficed to alter English so radically that if a tenth-century Englishman and a twentieth-century Englishman or American could meet face to face, they would not understand each other at all." Some changes are mild and lead to words which are similar in sound and in meaning, often indicating a common origin. Examples of such *cognates* are the English "father," the German "Vater," and the Latin "pater." Other changes have led to *non-cognates*, such as "equus" in Latin and "cheval" in French, corresponding to the English "horse." Words can be lost completely and new words can come into use. And the study of language change is not made easier by the fact that writing itself is a relatively recent event in the history of man's use of language.

A branch of linguistics called *glottochronology* has developed in recent years to study the loss of words from the vocabulary of a language and the possibility of dating various events in the evolution of languages. The rate of replacement of vocabulary is studied and the percentage of basic vocabulary still shared by two presently distinct but related languages is used to estimate how long ago they ceased being a single language and began diverging. Our aim is to present a probabilistic model and derive some formulas for this analysis. The subject is complex, research is ongoing, and the method has provoked much controversy in the anthropological and linguistic communities. Let the reader keep in mind as our simplifying assumptions are made that the complexity of the subject is better captured in models and methods of analysis more sophisticated than the one we present. References to the literature of glottochronology are given at the end of this unit as a guide for further study.

2. A "Death" Process for Words

Although our interest is in dating the divergence time of two related languages, let us begin by analyzing the changes in a single language. Suppose one constructs a list of basic meanings referring to such common objects, situations, or actions for which every community, regardless of culture or environment, has words. Examples of such universal cultural meanings, expressed for convenience by English words and taken from a list prepared by Swadesh [20], are "animal," "blood," "three," "to eat," "to die." In any language, each meaning in this basic list is expressed by a single word at each point of time. As time goes by, the language evolves and some of these words are replaced. We shall say a word "dies" if it is replaced by a non-cognate word and "lives" otherwise. Let us suppose there are N words in this basic list to begin with (at $t = 0$). Imagine keeping track of the words as time passes and denote by X_t the number of words still alive (i.e., unreplaced by non-cognates) at time $t > 0$. The death of words is regarded as a *random (stochastic) process** about which we make the following assumptions:

The process starts at time 0 with N words. During any short time interval of length h, each word has probability $\lambda h + o(h)$ to die, where $o(h)$ denotes a quantity of smaller order of magnitude than h, i.e., a quantity such that $\frac{o(h)}{h} \to 0$ as $h \to 0$. (The constant $\lambda > 0$ is a measure of the rate of decrease of the live word population: the larger λ, the greater the probability that a word dies and the faster the population of live words diminishes in size.) We assume no interaction among words. Then if there are n words alive at time t, the conditional probability of one death occurring between t and $t+h$ is $n\lambda h + o(h)$, the conditional probability of no death in $(t, t+h)$ is $1 - n\lambda h + o(h)$, and the conditional probability of more than one death in $(t, t+h)$ is $o(h)$.**

Letting

$$P_n(t) = \Pr(X_t = n), \tag{1}$$

we now show that these assumptions imply

$$P_n(t) = \binom{N}{n} e^{-\lambda n t} (1 - e^{-\lambda t})^{N-n} \qquad n = 0, 1, \dots, N. \tag{2}$$

To prove this, we first derive a system of differential equations for the probabilities $P_n(t)$ and then solve these to get the explicit formulas in (2).

---

*The main consequence of the probabilistic model that follows is the exponential decrease over time of the average number of words still alive. Those who prefer on first reading to avoid the mathematical analysis and concentrate on the application to language dating can skip directly to equation (7).

**These assumptions are familiar for the Yule process although our formulas will look a bit different since they are formulated for a stochastic process of pure death rather than pure birth type. See Feller [7] or Bailey [1] for a discussion of these processes. Our terminology (words "living" and "dying") is suggested by the usual applications to the growth of populations, where births and deaths of individuals rather than words are studied. The pure death process is used for the study of language changes in Brainerd [3].

Assume $n < N$ and observe the population of words at time $t + h$. The event that there are exactly n words alive at $t + h$ has probability $P_n(t+h)$ and can occur in three mutually exclusive ways: (1) at time t there are n words alive and no deaths occur between t and $t + h$; (2) at time t there are $n + 1$ words alive and one death occurs between t and $t + h$; (3) at time t there are $n + k$ words alive $(2 \leq k \leq N - n)$ and k deaths occur between t and $t + h$. The probability for (1) is $P_n(t)[1 - n\lambda h + o(h)]$, by our assumptions; the probability for (2) is $P_{n+1}(t)[(n + 1)\lambda h + o(h)]$; the probability for (3) is $\sum_{k=2}^{N-n} P_{n+k}(t)[o(h)]$. Noting that the product of any constant (in particular, a function not dependent on h) times a quantity that is $o(h)$ is again $o(h)$ and that the sum of a finite number of $o(h)$ quantities is also $o(h)$, we can verify that

$$P_n(t + h) = P_n(t)[1 - n\lambda h] + P_{n+1}(t)[(n + 1)\lambda h] + o(h).$$

This can be written in the form

$$\frac{P_n(t + h) - P_n(t)}{h} = -n\lambda P_n(t) + (n + 1)\lambda P_{n+1}(t) + \frac{o(h)}{h}.$$

As $h \to 0$, the last term has limit zero. Hence the limit of the left-hand side, which we recognize as the derivative $P'_n(t)$, exists and

$$P'_n(t) = -\lambda n P_n(t) + \lambda(n + 1)P_{n+1}(t) \qquad n = 0, 1, \ldots, N - 1. \qquad (3)$$

The case $n = N$ is special since the only way one can have all N words alive at time $t + h$ is by having N words alive at time t and no deaths in $(t, t + h)$. Therefore

$$P_N(t + h) = P_N(t)[1 - N\lambda h + o(h)]$$

which leads to

$$P'_N(t) = -\lambda N P_N(t). \qquad (4)$$

Our claim is that the functions $P_n(t)$ given by (2) are the solutions of the system of ordinary differential equations (3) and (4) provided we add the *initial conditions*

$$P_n(0) = \begin{cases} 0 & \text{if } n = 0, 1, \ldots, N - 1 \\ 1 & \text{if } n = N \end{cases} \qquad (5)$$

expressing the fact that we started with N words at time 0.

Solving the differential equation (4) together with the initial condition $P_N(0) = 1$, we get

$$P_N(t) = e^{-\lambda N t}.$$

Substituting this into (3) with $n = N - 1$, we have to determine $P_{N-1}(t)$ from a linear first-order differential equation with constant coefficients:

$$P'_{N-1}(t) + \lambda(N - 1)P_{N-1}(t) = \lambda N e^{-\lambda N t}.$$

Multiplying by the *integrating factor* $e^{\lambda(N-1)t}$ (see any differential equations textbook for this important technique) the equation becomes

$$[P_{N-1}(t)e^{\lambda(N-1)t}]' = \lambda N e^{-\lambda t}.$$

Integrating, then using the initial condition (5) to evaluate the constant of integration, we obtain

$$P_{N-1}(t) = N e^{-\lambda(N-1)t}(1 - e^{-\lambda t}).$$

This we easily check agrees with (2) when $n = N - 1$. Continuing in the same way, or more rigorously by using backward induction (Exercise 1), the solution (2) is established. (Another way of solving the system of ordinary differential equations (3) and (4), using *generating functions* and reducing the system to a single partial differential equation, is discussed by Bailey [1] and outlined in Exercise 2.)

The solution (2) has the form

$$\binom{N}{n}p^n(1 - p)^{N-n} = b_n, \text{ say,} \tag{6}$$

where $p = e^{-\lambda t}$. These probabilities are recognized as the *binomial distribution*. It will be helpful to summarize some facts about these probabilities from elementary probability theory.

Lemma. Let an experiment consist of N independent trials on each of which an event either occurs, with probability p, $0 < p < 1$, or does not occur, with probability $1 - p$. Then the probability of the event occurring exactly n times in the N-trial experiment is given by b_n in (6). Furthermore, the mean (or expected value of the) number of times the event occurs, defined by $\sum_{n=0}^{N} n b_n$, equals Np.

It follows from (2) and this Lemma that

$$E(X_t) = N e^{-\lambda t}, \tag{7}$$

i.e., *on the average the number of words remaining unchanged decreases exponentially with time*. (See Exercise 3 for a different derivation of (7) that does *not* require the explicit solution of the system of differential equations (3) and (4) and thus makes no use of the binomial distribution.) The same exponential decay is familiar for the decomposition of a radioactive substance. In fact, equation (7) is referred to as "morpheme decay." (For our purposes, the linguistic term "morpheme" can be replaced by "word.") It is customary to take 1000 years (one millenium) as the unit of time. From (7),

$$e^{-\lambda} = \frac{E(X_1)}{N} = k, \text{ say.}$$

The quantity k is the average number of words alive (i.e., not replaced by non-cognates) in one millenium. Linguists have studied many languages and their changes over time. Table 1, adapted from Lees [15], shows for thirteen languages the estimated value of k, the proportion of words alive at $t = 1$.

Language	Proportion k of Words Alive per Millenium
1. English	.766
2. Spanish	.790
3. French	.776
4. German	.854
5. Coptic	.760
6. Athenian	.836
7. Cypriote	.829
8. Chinese	.795
9. Swedish	.854
10. Italian	.839
11. Portuguese	.806
12. Rumanian	.764
13. Catalan	.793

Table 1. Morpheme decay, after Lees [15, p.118].

Lees used a basic list of 215 English words and obtained the most common colloquial terms of each language at an older and again at a more recent stage of its development. The two stages were able to be dated independently. Corresponding morphemes were compared to determine the proportion of cognate word pairs shared by the two stages. The values of k were then calculated for the standard time unit of one millenium.

The evidence in Table 1 suggests a certain similarity among languages, but linguists agree that the replacement rate λ and hence k varies not only from language to language but from meaning to meaning within a single language. Recent work of Dyen, James, and Cole [6] and Kruskal, Dyen, and Black [13,14] takes account of the variation in λ, but we shall follow the early writers by ignoring this variation. In fact, we assume from now on that

$$e^{-\lambda} = k = .8, \tag{8}$$

the average of the values of k in Table 1. (Actually, these k-values have mean .805 and standard deviation .03.) As Lees [15, p.119] optimistically summarized his data: "We take this to mean that on the average about 80% of the basic-root-morphemes of a language will survive as cognates after 1000 years, for all languages, at all time."

3. Comparing Cognates in Two Languages

Now we come to the comparison of two related languages and the estimate of their date of divergence from a common source language. The splitting of one language into two surely occurs over a considerable period of time and interaction between users of the developing languages must be the rule rather than the exception. Nevertheless, the simplifying assumptions are made that the separation occurred at a particular moment in time and that the two emerging languages develop independently from that moment on. We can do no better than quote Kruskal, Dyen, and Black [13, p.367]: "However, our assumptions are good enough so that we can learn a good deal. With the aid of what we learn, we will be able to improve the assumptions. Use of partly true ideas as a tool for further learning is a classic method in science."

With a list of basic meanings before us, we see what words in each of the two languages being compared are used for each meaning. Some of these will be cognates representing words from the common source that have not been transformed, that are still "alive" in our terminology. Others will have "died" with non-cognates appearing in their place in the two languages. Starting with N items in the list of basic meanings, we let S_t denote the *number of words shared as cognates in the two languages after time t from the moment of separation.*

The probability that a given word in one of the languages is still alive at time t is $e^{-\lambda t}$. (This can be seen directly from (2) by putting $N = 1$ and noting that $P_1(t) = e^{-\lambda t}$.) Since the two languages are assumed to develop independently and with the same value of the parameter λ, the probability that the words in both languages for a given basic meaning are shared (i.e., both are "alive") is $(e^{-\lambda t})^2$ or $e^{-2\lambda t}$. The N meanings in the list form N independent trials, each leading to success (corresponding words in the languages are cognates) or to failure (corresponding words are non-cognates). Hence, according to the Lemma, we are led to the binomial distribution for the random variable S_t. By (6),

$$\Pr(S_t = s) = \binom{N}{s} e^{-2\lambda st}(1 - e^{-2\lambda t})^{N-s} \qquad s = 0, 1, \ldots, N. \quad (9)$$

Now at a certain known date but of course an unknown value of t, a linguist analyzes the two languages using a given list of N basic meanings and determines an empirical value, say s_e, for S_t. Is there a way to estimate the corresponding value of the separation time t? We argue as follows. The probability of obtaining the experimental value s_e is given by (9) with $s = s_e$. This probability depends on the unknown value of t since all other quantities (N and λ) are assumed fixed and known. Let us choose as our estimate of t that value which makes the probability of obtaining the actual experimental outcome s_e as large as possible. This is the important method of *maximum likelihood estimation*. (See Mood, Graybill, and Boes [17, p.276 ff.] for a full discussion and Exercises 4–6 for additional applications.)

Our estimation procedure is therefore as follows: Set $s = s_e$ in (9) and find the value of the separation time t, say $\hat{t}$, for which $\Pr(S_t = s_e)$ is maximized. Then $\hat{t}$ is the maximum likelihood estimate for t. It is easier (and we get the same value for $\hat{t}$) if we maximize the logarithm of the probability rather than the probability itself. Now

$$\log \Pr(S_t = s_e) = \log \binom{N}{s_e} - 2\lambda s_e t + (N - s_e)\log(1 - e^{-2\lambda t}).$$

Differentiating and setting the derivative equal to zero, we have

$$-2\lambda s_e + (N - s_e)\frac{2\lambda e^{-2\lambda t}}{1 - e^{-2\lambda t}} = 0,$$

and solving for t yields

$$\hat{t} = \frac{-\log(s_e/N)}{2\lambda}. \tag{10}$$

(We leave for the reader the verification, by the second derivative test or otherwise, that this does indeed supply a maximum value.) Since we have assumed in (8) that $e^{-\lambda} = k = .8$, we have $\lambda = .223$ and so our estimate for the separation time of the two languages is

$$\hat{t} = -(2.24)\log(s_e/N). \tag{11}$$

The fraction (s_e/N) is the experimentally observed proportion of the N pairs of test words which are shared (cognates) in the two languages. Although other more favorable results are available, let us conclude with data from Lees [15] on the comparison of Modern German and Modern English. He found 124 cognates (58.5%) in a total of 212 comparisons. By means of equation (11),

$$\hat{t} = -(2.24)\log(.585) = 1.2 \text{ millenia},$$

or, counting back from the year of Lees' work, about the year 750 A.D. This estimate is too late by several centuries since the Germanic invasions of Britain began about 450 A.D.

Two observations seem appropriate at this point. First, a very rough calculation can be used to check that the value $\hat{t} = 1.2$ is about what should be expected from our theory. We have assumed that $k = 80\%$

of the basic words survive as cognates after one millenium. For two languages developing independently we therefore would expect 64% of the basic words to survive after one millenium. Even linear extrapolation then produces approximately 1.2 millenia as the elapsed time corresponding to Lees' observed survival value of 58.5%.

Second, the 300-year discrepancy in our estimate can easily be made up if the value of k, taken as .8 in our derivation, is raised to some value between .83 and .84. (A glance at Table 1 shows that the value of k for German was .854.) The sensitivity of the value of $\hat{t}$ to the assumed value of k reinforces the need for more sophisticated analyses that take into account the variation in k among languages and also among basic meanings within a single language [6, 13, 14].

The oversimplified model we have presented will perhaps serve as an incentive for further study by interested readers. For a flavor of some of the controversy surrounding glottochronology, see Chretien [4] and van der Merwe [21]. The former's misunderstandings are dealt with by Dobson, Kruskal, Sankoff, and Savage [5] and the latter's contribution is followed by comments from 17 critics, some friendly and others less so. An earlier contribution by Bergsland and Vogt [2] also is accompanied by numerous commentaries. Early references can be found in Gudschinsky [8], and an article by Hymes [12] summarizes developments up to 1960. Much of the early literature dealt with deterministic rather than stochastic models. For the latter, see Brainerd [3] and Sankoff [19]. In the work of Kruskal, Dyen, and Black [13, 14] one finds powerful computer techniques and new methods of data analysis brought to bear on the problems of reconstructing language trees. Guy [9] uses computer simulation to study the lexical diversification of language families. In another monograph [10], he uses computer techniques to count sound correspondences between words in two languages and explores the possibility of producing phylogenetic classifications based not on the commonly used proportions of shared cognates, but rather on measures of language similarity obtained from tables of such sound correspondences.

Exercises

1. Use backward induction to prove rigorously that the probabilities $P_n(t)$ given by (2) are the solutions of the system of differential equations (3) and (4) with initial conditions (5).

2. To solve the system of differential equations (3) and (4) with initial conditions (5) by the method of generating functions, proceed as follows.

   Step 1. Define the generating function

   $$G(s,t) = \sum_{n=0}^{N} P_n(t)s^n.$$

Note that

$$\frac{\partial G}{\partial s} = \sum_{n=1}^{N} P_n(t)ns^{n-1}, \quad \frac{\partial G}{\partial t} = \sum_{n=0}^{N} P'_n(t)s^n$$

and use (3) and (4) to show that

$$\lambda(s-1)\frac{\partial G}{\partial s} + \frac{\partial G}{\partial t} = 0. \tag{12}$$

Show further that the initial conditions (5) imply

$$G(s,0) = s^N. \tag{13}$$

This step has thus transformed the problem of solving a system of ordinary differential-difference equations to that of solving a single partial differential equation.

Step 2. Use a result from the theory of partial differential equations to show that the general solution of (12) is given by

$$G(s,t) = \Psi\left(\frac{e^{\lambda t}}{s-1}\right)$$

where Ψ is an arbitrary function.*

Step 3. Use the initial condition (13) to show that

$$\Psi(w) = (1 + \frac{1}{w})^N$$

and hence that

$$G(s,t) = (1 - e^{-\lambda t} + se^{-\lambda t})^N. \tag{14}$$

Step 4. From the definition of the generating function, observe that $P_n(t)$ is the coefficient of s^n in $G(s,t)$. (This is the sense in which the function G *generates* the sequence of probabilities $\{P_n(t)\}$.) Note from (14) that $G(s,t)$ is of the form $(a+b)^N$ and use the binomial expansion to show that

$$P_n(t) = \binom{N}{n}\left(e^{-\lambda t}\right)^n\left(1 - e^{-\lambda t}\right)^{N-n},$$

the familiar solution given by (2).

---

*See Martin and Reissner [16, pp.255–265] for a discussion of the partial differential equation $P\frac{\partial z}{\partial x} + Q\frac{\partial z}{\partial y} = R$ where P, Q, and R are functions of x, y, and z. The result needed here is the special case $R = 0$.

3. The derivative of $E(X_t)$ in (7) was based on the explicit solution of the system of differential equations (3) and (4) with initial conditions (5). Here is an alternative method of finding $E(X_t)$ *without* first solving the differential equations. Let

$$E(X_t) = \sum_{k=0}^{N} k P_k(t) = m_1(t), \text{ say,}$$

and

$$E(X_t^2) = \sum_{k=0}^{N} k^2 P_k(t) = m_2(t), \text{ say.}$$

Differentiate m_1 and use (3) and (4) to show that

$$m_1'(t) = -\lambda m_1(t). \tag{15}$$

Note that the initial conditions (5) imply $m_1(0) = N$. Solve the simple differential equation (15) with this initial condition to show that

$$m_1(t) = N e^{-\lambda t},$$

as in (7).

4. Consider n Bernoulli trials (think of coin tosses) with probability of success equal to p on each trial. Let X denote the total number of successes. Then X is binomially distributed, i.e.,

$$\Pr(X = k) = \binom{n}{k} p^k (1-p)^{n-k} \quad k = 0, 1, \ldots, n.$$

Suppose n such trials result in exactly r successes. Show that $\hat{p}$, the maximum likelihood estimate of p, is given by $\hat{p} = r/n$, the proportion of successes obtained among the n trials.

Hint. As in the text, it is easier to maximize the logarithm of the likelihood $\Pr(X = r)$ rather than the likelihood itself.

5. In the text, we noted that the random variable S_t is binomially distributed with $p = e^{-2\lambda t}$ and $n = N$ trials. According to the previous exercise, the maximum likelihood estimate of p is given by s_e/N. Using the so-called invariance principle for maximum likelihood estimators (if $\hat{\Theta}$ is the maximum likelihood estimator of Θ, then $h(\hat{\Theta})$ is the maximum likelihood estimator of $h(\Theta)$, provided h has an inverse), show that the maximum likelihood estimate of t is given by

$$\hat{t} = \frac{-\log(s_e/N)}{2\lambda},$$

thus supplying another derivation of (10).

6. A coin with probability p for heads is tossed until the first head occurs. Suppose k tosses are required. Show that the maximum likelihood estimate of p is $1/k$.

7. Consider the words corresponding to the list of N basic meanings in a single language. Equation (2) gives the (binomial) probability that n of these words are still alive at time t. Suppose that $N = 100$, $k = e^{-\lambda} = .8$, and $t = 1$. From equation (7) we know that the expected or mean value of X_1, the number of words still alive after one millenium, is 80. Using a table of binomial probabilities, verify that this number of words alive (a) is the most probable value of the random variable X_1, but (b) nevertheless has probability only 0.099.

8. Suppose two languages L_1 and L_2 evolve, starting at $t = 0$, independently from the same parent language. Let $X_1(1) = X_2(1) = 80$, i.e., each language has exactly 80 words (corresponding to a list of $N = 100$ basic meanings) that are still "alive" at time $t = 1$. Then S_1, the number of words the two languages still have in common as cognates, depends on the particular words lost. If L_1 and L_2 lost exactly the same 20 words, they will have 80 words in common. At the other extreme, if the two sets of words that have "died" do not overlap at all, then L_1 and L_2 will have only 60 words in common. Assume $e^{-\lambda} = k = .8$ for each language, implying that an average of 20 words die in each language in one millenium.

(a) Show that $E(S_1) = 64$ words.

(b) Given the result of part (a), we ask how likely it is in the situation considered here for L_1 and L_2 to have 64 words in common. Show that

$$\Pr(S_1 = 64 \mid X_1(1) = X_2(1) = 80) = \frac{\binom{80}{64}\binom{20}{16}}{\binom{100}{80}} = .24.$$

(c) Calculate $p_s = \Pr(S_1 = s \mid X_1(1) = X_2(1) = 80)$ for $s = 60, 61,$ ..., 68 (these leading to values of p_s at least .01 to two decimal places) and thus verify the entries in the following table:

s	60	61	62	63	64	65	66	67	68
p_s	.01	.05	.11	.19	.24	.22	.13	.04	.01

(d) From the values in (c), calculate the mean value of S_1.

9. Assume two languages L_1 and L_2 evolve independently from the same parent language, starting at time $t = 0$. Let $X_i(t)$ denote the number of words (corresponding to a list of N basic meanings) that are still alive in language L_i at time t . Suppose the number of words shared as cognates in L_1 and L_2 at time t is S_t. Show that

$$\Pr(S_t = s \mid X_1(t) = j,\, X_2(t) = k) = \frac{\dbinom{j}{s}\dbinom{N-j}{k-s}}{\dbinom{N}{k}}.$$

(Formulas of this sort appear in Chretien [4, p.18] and Brainerd [3, p.77].)

Bibliography

1. Bailey, N. T. J., *The Elements of Stochastic Processes with Applications to the Natural Sciences*, New York: Wiley, 1964.

2. Bergsland, K. and H. Vogt, "On the Validity of Glottochronology," *Current Anthropology*, vol. 3 (1962), 115–129. Comments by various authors (pp.129–148) and reply by the authors (pp.148–152).

3. Brainerd, B., "A Stochastic Process Related to Language Change," *Journal of Applied Probability*, vol. 7 (1970), 69–78.

4. Chretien, C. D., "The Mathematical Models of Glottochronology," *Language*, vol. 38 (1962), 11–37.

5. Dobson, A. J., J. B. Kruskal, D. Sankoff, and L. J. Savage, "The Mathematics of Glottochronology Revisited," *Anthropological Linguistics*, vol. 14 (1972), 205–212.

6. Dyen, I., A. T. James, and J. W. L. Cole, "Language Divergence and Estimated Word Retention Rate," *Language*, vol. 43 (1967), 150–171.

7. Feller, W., *An Introduction to Probability Theory and Its Applications*, vol. 1, third edition, New York: Wiley, 1968.

8. Gudschinsky, S. C., "The ABC's of Lexicostatistics (Glottochronology)," *Word*, vol. 12 (1956), 175–210.

9. Guy, J. B. M., *Experimental Glottochronology: Basic Methods and Results*, Pacific Linguistics Series B, Monograph No. 75, Canberra: Australian National University, 1980.

10. Guy, J. B. M., *Glottochronology Without Cognate Recognition*, Pacific Linguistics Series B, Monograph No. 79, Canberra: Australian National University, 1980.

11. Hockett, C. F., *A Course in Modern Linguistics*, New York: Macmillan, 1958.

12. Hymes, D., "Lexicostatistics So Far," *Current Anthropology*, vol. 1 (1960), 3–43, 338–345.

13. Kruskal, J. B., I. Dyen, and P. Black, "The Vocabulary Method of Reconstructing Language Trees: Innovations and Large Scale Applications," pp.361–380 in Hodson, F. R., D. G. Kendall, and P. Tautu (Eds.), *Mathematics in the Archaeological and Historical Sciences*, Edinburgh: Edinburgh University Press, 1971.

14. Kruskal, J. B., I. Dyen, and P. Black, "Some Results from the Vocabulary Method of Reconstructing Language Trees," pp.30–55 in Dyen, I. (Ed.), *Lexicostatistics in Genetic Linguistics*, The Hague: Mouton, 1973.

15. Lees, R. B., "The Basis of Glottochronology," *Language*, vol. 29 (1953), 113–127.

16. Martin, W. T. and E. Reissner, *Elementary Differential Equations*, second edition, Reading, Mass.: Addison-Wesley, 1961.

17. Mood, A. M., F. A. Graybill, and D. C. Boes, *Introduction to the Theory of Statistics*, third edition, New York: McGraw-Hill, 1974.

18. Sankoff, D., "Mathematical Developments in Lexicostatistic Theory," pp.93–113 in Sebeok, T. A. (Ed.), *Current Trends in Linguistics*, vol. 11, The Hague: Mouton, 1973.

19. Sankoff, D., "Reconstructing the History and Geography of an Evolutionary Tree," *American Mathematical Monthly*, vol. 79 (1972), 596–603.

20. Swadesh, M., "Lexico-Statistic Dating of Prehistoric Ethnic Contacts," *Proceedings of the American Philosophical Society*, vol. 96 (1952), 452–463.

21. van der Merwe, N. J., "New Mathematics for Glottochronology," *Current Anthropology*, vol. 7 (1966), 485–488. See Comments on pp.488–500.

Chapter 6
Probability Models for Mobility

1. The Basic BKM Markov Model

We are a mobile society. Movement up the social ladder, movement among occupations and ranks in employment, movement from one residential location to another are all routine. It is not surprising that mobility has been studied at great length by social scientists, especially by sociologists, economists, and demographers. Many probability models have been introduced in an attempt to understand the possible dynamics of the observed transition process among social, occupational, income, or geographic states followed by subjects in studies of social, occupational, income, or geographic mobility. One seeks some reasonably concise set of assumptions of how people behave that will fit experimentally obtained mobility data. As we shall see, the simplest Markov chain model assuming a homogeneous population produces theoretical projections that deviate significantly from observed values. Much subsequent research was therefore focused on developing ways to accommodate population heterogeneity. Our aim here is to survey a small part of this work, following a line of research initiated by Blumen, Kogan, and McCarthy (BKM) [3] in their study of intragenerational labor mobility.

These authors studied quarterly data for the years 1947–49 obtained from a sample of all workers who, according to the files of the Bureau of Old Age and Survivor Insurance, were in covered employment since the inception of the social security system in 1937. Workers were distinguished by sex and age (only age groups 20–24, 40–44, 60–64 were sampled) and industries were coded into eleven categories. For example, one category included all those in agricultural farms, forestry, and fisheries, another included all workers in banks, insurance, and real estate, and the eleventh category was set aside for those who were unemployed. Each person's work category was recorded for each quarterly period and the resulting pattern of labor mobility was the object of the study.

A brief review of the simplest probability model considered by BKM will help establish some key ideas and notation. Time is a discrete variable with 0 as the initial time and successive periods (quarters in BKM) labeled $1, 2, 3, \ldots$. An individual is located at any time in exactly one of the possible states (work categories in BKM) numbered $1, 2, \ldots, N$ ($N = 11$ in BKM). The essential requirement of a model is that it specify the way in which

79

changes in state occur. Let us assume these are governed by *transition probabilities* which are independent of time. Let p_{ij} denote the probability that a worker ends up in state j after a single time period, given he is in state i at the beginning of the period. Since i and j vary from 1 to N, there are N^2 transition probabilities in all and these are arranged in an $N \times N$ *transition probability matrix*

$$
P = \begin{pmatrix}
p_{11} & p_{12} & \cdots & p_{1N} \\
p_{21} & p_{22} & \cdots & p_{2N} \\
\vdots & \vdots & & \vdots \\
p_{N1} & p_{N2} & \cdots & p_{NN}
\end{pmatrix}. \tag{1}
$$

This matrix has nonnegative entries, of course. Its row sums equal 1 since a worker, starting from any state, must end up in exactly one of the N possible states after one period of time. In symbols, for $i, j = 1, 2, \ldots, N$,

$$
\sum_{j=1}^{N} p_{ij} = 1, \qquad p_{ij} \geq 0.
$$

Let $f_i^{(n)}$ denote the probability that a worker is in state i at time n. These *state probabilities at time n* are conveniently arranged in a row-vector

$$
\mathbf{f}^{(n)} = (f_1^{(n)} f_2^{(n)} \cdots f_N^{(n)}) \tag{2}
$$

known as the *state probability vector at time n*. (These vectors, for $n = 0, 1, 2, \ldots$, have nonnegative entries whose sum is 1.) We shall assume the initial state probability vector $\mathbf{f}^{(0)}$ is given. This vector specifies the initial distribution of workers among the occupational categories. The transition probability matrix P specifies the way in which transitions from one work category to another take place from one time period to the next.

The matrix P and vector $\mathbf{f}^{(0)}$ together define a *Markov chain* with states $1, 2, \ldots, N$. The theory of Markov chains is well developed and only some basic results without proofs are included here. Many references, at various levels of difficulty and comprehensiveness, are available for further study. One can consult sections on Markov chains in such texts for beginners as Chung [7], Snell [43], Maki and Thompson [27], and Gaver and Thompson [12]. Among the many references at a more advanced level, we suggest the appropriate chapters in Feller [10] or Bhat [2], as well as the more comprehensive books by Chung [6], Isaacson and Madsen [20], and Kemeny and Snell [22].

One more bit of notation is needed. Let $p_{ij}^{(n)}$ denote the *n-step transition probability* of going from state i to state j. That is, $p_{ij}^{(n)}$ is the conditional probability that a worker ends up in state j at time n given he starts in state i at time 0. (The transition probability p_{ij} already defined is the one-step transition probability $p_{ij}^{(1)}$, but the superscript is suppressed for convenience.) In the same way that the p_{ij} form the matrix P, the probabilities $p_{ij}^{(n)}$ are arranged in a matrix denoted $P^{(n)}$, the *n-step transition probability matrix*.

From the theory of Markov chains, the following results will be needed.

Result 1. To go from state i to state j in n steps, one must go from state i to one of the N states, say k, in one step and then go from state k to state j in the remaining $n - 1$ steps. Hence

$$p_{ij}^{(n)} = \sum_{k=1}^{N} p_{ik} p_{kj}^{(n-1)}$$

or, in matrix notation, for $n = 2, 3, \ldots,$

$$P^{(n)} = P P^{(n-1)}.$$

By repeated application of this recursive equation, we have

$$P^{(n)} = P^n, \tag{3}$$

i.e., the n-step transition probability matrix is the nth power of the one-step transition probability matrix.

Result 2. To be in state j at time n requires being in one of the N states, say i, at time $n-1$ and then moving from state i to state j in the remaining time period. Hence

$$f_j^{(n)} = \sum_{i=1}^{N} f_i^{(n-1)} p_{ij}$$

or, in vector-matrix notation, for $n = 1, 2, \ldots,$

$$\mathbf{f}^{(n)} = \mathbf{f}^{(n-1)} P. \tag{4}$$

Repeated application of this recursive equation yields

$$\mathbf{f}^{(n)} = \mathbf{f}^{(0)} P^n. \tag{5}$$

In words: to find the vector of probabilities with which the various states are occupied at time n, the corresponding state probability vector at the initial time 0 is multiplied by the nth power of the transition probability matrix.

Result 3. Suppose P is a *regular* matrix, i.e., either P itself or some power of P has all *positive* entries. (This condition is not necessary for the result to follow, but it is an acceptable and convenient sufficient condition. See the discussion in McFarland [30, p.469,472].) Then as $n \to \infty$,

$$P^n \to W \tag{6}$$

where the matrix W has the following properties:

(a) W has identical rows, each equal to a vector $\mathbf{w} = (w_1 w_2 \ldots w_N)$, whose entries are positive and add to 1, i.e.,

$$w_i > 0 \quad \text{and} \quad \sum_{i=1}^{N} w_i = 1. \tag{7}$$

(b) The row-vector $\mathbf{w}$ is the unique *fixed-point probability vector* associated with the transition probability matrix P. This means $\mathbf{w}$ is the only vector whose components satisfy (7) and which is a solution of the system of equations given by

$$\mathbf{w} = \mathbf{w}P. \tag{8}$$

(Satisfying (7) makes $\mathbf{w}$ a *probability* vector. Satisfying (8) makes $\mathbf{w}$ a *fixed-point* vector of P, since post-multiplying $\mathbf{w}$ by P leaves $\mathbf{w}$ fixed.)

(c) As the number of transitions increases, we have

$$\lim_{n \to \infty} f_i^{(n)} = w_i \tag{9}$$

or, in vector notation,

$$\mathbf{f}^{(n)} \to \mathbf{w}. \tag{10}$$

This follows readily (Exercise 1) from (5) and (6), together with Result 3(a), but it has an important interpretation. The limiting value w_i is the *long-run equilibrium* (sometimes referred to as *steady state* or *invariant*) probability of finding a worker in occupational category i. Note the fact, typical of Markov theory, that this *long-run equilibrium probability does not depend on the initial state probability vector* $\mathbf{f}^{(0)}$. In practical applications, one finds that after a sufficient passage of time, the probability of being in any particular state depends only on the various transition probabilities and not on the initial state. In view of (8), this long-run probability distribution of being in the various states is stable or unchanging as the process continues. (But see Feller [10, p.395] for a discussion of the subtle meaning of this equilibrium condition.)

Before returning to the BKM labor mobility study, it will be helpful to list three crucial assumptions made in developing the Markov chain model just outlined. First, there is *stationarity*, i.e., the assumption that the transition probabilities are constant over time, that the same transition probability matrix P governs the movement of workers among work categories in every time period. Second, there is the so-called *Markov hypothesis*, i.e., the assumption that a worker's transition probability p_{ij} depends only on his current work category (state i) and not on the history of past moves leading to his present state. Third, there is the assumption of population *homogeneity*, i.e., that all workers have the same transition probability matrix P. (These assumptions are too restrictive and unrealistic and are relaxed in subsequent studies.)

It is the homogeneity assumption that allowed BKM to use the *proportion* of all sampled workers making a given transition as an estimate of the corresponding transition probability. In this way they estimated the entries in the transition probability matrix P, obtaining a matrix $\hat{P}$ as their estimate. By (3) we know that higher-order transition probability matrices are powers of the first-order matrix $\hat{P}$. Hence the theory predicts that after eight quarters, say, transitions should be governed by $\hat{P}^8$. But transitions of workers in the sample from the initial time to eight quarters later are recorded in the data and hence a comparison is possible between the transition probabilities actually observed and those predicted by $\hat{P}^8$ according to the Markov model.

Work Category	1	2	3	4	5	6	7	8	9	10	11
Predicted from $\hat{P}^8$	.217	.277	.412	.526	.568	.452	.427	.423	.242	.006	.293
Observed	.500	.649	.681	.749	.749	.756	.693	.745	.573	.013	.526

Table 1. Comparison of diagonal elements from expected and observed eighth-order matrices for males 40–44. Data from BKM [3, Table 4.8].

Table 1 summarizes one small part of such a comparison, recording only main diagonal elements or proportions remaining in the same work category after 8 periods. Notice that the diagonal elements of $\hat{P}^8$ underestimate the observed proportions. The Markov model predicts more "moving" than actually occurred and therefore less "staying" than the observed data. Another test of the Markov BKM theory using occupational mobility data was carried out by Mahoney and Milkovich [26].

2. The Stayer-Mover Model

The significant discrepancy between data and theory has led to numerous modifications of the simple Markov chain mobility model. In BKM [3] one finds the so-called *Stayer-Mover model* in which the homogeneity assumption is modified and it is no longer assumed that all workers have the same transition probability matrix. Now workers are of two types: *Movers* who each have the same regular transition probability matrix denoted now by M, and *Stayers* who have as transition matrix the $N \times N$ identity matrix I with 1's on the main diagonal and 0's elsewhere, i.e., who are *sure* to stay in the same work category from period to period.

Let us define the $N \times N$ diagonal matrix

$$S = \begin{pmatrix} s_1 & 0 & \ldots & 0 \\ 0 & s_2 & \ldots & 0 \\ \vdots & \vdots & & \vdots \\ 0 & 0 & \ldots & s_n \end{pmatrix} \tag{11}$$

where s_i is the initial fraction of workers in state i who are Stayers. Now we find

$$p_{ij} = \begin{cases} (s_i)(1) + (1 - s_i)m_{ii} & \text{if } j = i \\ (1 - s_i)m_{ij} & \text{if } j \sim i \end{cases}$$

since a worker starting in state i can end up after one period in the same state i in two ways: he is a Stayer and is sure to remain in state i or he is a Mover and has probability m_{ii} to remain. In matrix notation, we write

$$P = S + (I - S)M. \tag{12}$$

Continuing, we find by analogous reasoning,

$$p_{ij}^{(2)} = \begin{cases} (s_i)(1) + (1 - s_i)m_{ii}^{(2)} & \text{if } j = i \\ (1 - s_i)m_{ij}^{(2)} & \text{if } j \sim i. \end{cases}$$

But M is a transition probability matrix and hence (by Result 1) two-step transitions of Movers are governed by M^2. Therefore

$$P^{(2)} = S + (I - S)M^2$$

and more generally, for each positive integer n,

$$P^{(n)} = S + (I - S)M^n. \tag{13}$$

By assumption, M is regular and so (by Result 3) $M^n \to V$ as $n \to \infty$, where V is a matrix with identical rows, each the fixed-point probability vector, say $\mathbf{v}$, associated with M, i.e., $\mathbf{v} = \mathbf{v}M$. But $S + (I - S)V$, the limiting matrix for all workers does *not* have identical rows as it did in the Markov chain model. Now,

$$\mathbf{f}^{(n)} = \mathbf{f}^{(0)}P^{(n)} \to \mathbf{f}^{(0)}[S + (I - S)V], \tag{14}$$

so the limiting probability that a worker starting in some work category ends up in a specified category *does* depend on the starting state.

Unknown parameters of the Stayer-Mover model are s_1, s_2, ..., s_N, the proportions of Stayers in the N work categories, and the transition probabilities m_{ij} of the Mover matrix M. Unlike the simple Markov chain model, these parameters cannot be estimated directly from longitudinal income data since an individual who stays in a given work category for two consecutive periods may be a Stayer or a Mover. Nevertheless, indirect methods of statistical estimation have been developed by Goodman [16]. BKM were able before this to obtain numerical estimates and once again compare predictions of the Stayer-Mover model with observed data.

Work Category	1	2	3	4	5	6	7	8	9	10	11
Predicted (Stayer-Mover)	.516	.648	.691	.760	.768	.755	.698	.747	.582	.016	.554
Observed	.500	.649	.681	.749	.749	.756	.693	.745	.573	.013	.526

Table 2. Comparison of diagonal elements from expected and observed eighth-order matrices for males 40–44. Data from BKM [3, Table 6.7].

In Table 2, the proportions remaining in the same work category after 8 periods are recorded. The extraordinary improvement in fit, as compared with Table 1 for the simple Markov chain model, is not as spectacular a success for BKM as one would think. For, as they themselves admit [3, p.131]:

... stayer-mover model underestimates the fraction of workers show-ing the same code group for quarters of fourth order, overestimates this fraction for quarters of eleventh order, and shows, on the whole, a random pattern for quarters of the eighth order. In other words, we have managed to "fit" the model to observed eighth order move-ment with fairly good results, but this "fit" does not hold up too well for either shorter or longer periods of time. We speak of "fitting" in this instance because our estimates of the matrices S and M depend fundamentally on the eighth order "observed" matrices.

3. Further Modifications

The basic theory has been modified in many ways in attempts to create more realistic models to explain observed mobility data. A few of these modifications are considered here.

Instead of each worker making exactly one transition in each time period, let us assume transitions occur randomly in time. Suppose for the moment that we consider only workers with the same average number of transitions, i.e., with the same *transition rate*, say $\lambda > 0$, per unit time interval. All transitions of these individuals, when they occur, are assumed to be governed by the same transition probability matrix M. Let $r_k(t)$ denote the probability that such an individual undergoes exactly k transitions in $(0,t)$ and suppose the number of transitions occurring in time t

is a random variable following a Poisson distribution*, i.e.,

$$r_k(t) = e^{-\lambda t}\frac{(\lambda t)^k}{k!} \quad k = 0, 1, 2, \ldots. \tag{15}$$

Now $P^{(1)}$, the transition matrix at time $t = 1$ is obtained by averaging, noting that if k transitions happen to occur in time 1 then M^k is the corresponding transition matrix. Hence

$$P^{(1)} = \sum_{k=0}^{\infty} r_k(1)M^k. \tag{16}$$

For time $t = n$, we have

$$\begin{aligned}
P^{(n)} &= \sum_{k=0}^{\infty} r_k(n)M^k \\
&= \sum_{k=0}^{\infty} e^{-\lambda n}\frac{(\lambda nM)^k}{k!} \\
&= e^{-\lambda n}e^{\lambda nM} = e^{-\lambda n(I-M)}.
\end{aligned}$$

Due to the exponential form, this result is the n-th power of the result when $n = 1$. That is,

$$P^{(n)} = [P^{(1)}]^n \tag{17}$$

which is the same as the Markov chain property (3). When transitions occur randomly in time according to a Poisson distribution and the population is homogeneous in its transition rate, this Markov property follows.

Now suppose we relax the unrealistic assumption that all workers have the same transition rate. In fact, let there be m types of workers differing in their transition rates, with a proportion f_i of all workers having transition rate λ_i. (Of course, $f_1 + f_2 + \cdots + f_m = 1$.) Reinterpreting $r_k(t)$ as the probability that a worker chosen at random from the entire population makes k transitions during $(0,t)$, we have

$$r_k(t) = \sum_{i=1}^{m} f_i e^{-\lambda_i t}\frac{(\lambda_i t)^k}{k!}. \tag{18}$$

Finally, suppose population heterogeneity is characterized not by a finite number of distinct groups each with its own transition rate, as in (18),

---

*Two different derivations of the Poisson distribution as a probabilistic description of "random events occurring in time" can be found in Feller [10, pp.156,446]. It is easy to verify that $r_k(t) > 0$ and $\sum_{k=0}^{\infty} r_k(t) = 1$ so (15) specifies a bona fide probability distribution. Also, the mean number of transitions in $(0,t)$ is given by the sum $\sum_{k=0}^{\infty} kr_k(t) = \lambda t$, so the mean number of transitions per unit time is λ, as claimed.

but rather by a transition rate that is a continuous random variable with probability density function f defined for $\lambda > 0$. Then (18) becomes

$$r_k(t) = \int_0^\infty f(\lambda)e^{-\lambda t}\frac{(\lambda t)^k}{k!}\,d\lambda. \tag{19}$$

Spilerman [45] assumes f is the *gamma density*,

$$f(\lambda) = \frac{b^a}{\Gamma(a)}\lambda^{a-1}e^{-b\lambda} \qquad \lambda > 0, \quad a > 0, \quad b > 0, \tag{20}$$

where

$$\Gamma(a) = \int_0^\infty x^{a-1}e^{-x}\,dx.$$

It is then a straightforward calculation (Exercise 4) to show that

$$r_k(t) = \binom{a+k-1}{k}\left(\frac{t}{b+t}\right)^k\left(\frac{b}{b+t}\right)^a, \tag{21}$$

so the number of transitions made by a random worker is distributed according to the so-called *negative binomial distribution*.*

Returning to (16) with $r_k(1)$ given by (21), we now have

$$P^{(1)} = \left(\frac{b}{b+1}\right)^a \sum_{k=0}^\infty (-1)^k\binom{-a}{k}\left(\frac{M}{b+1}\right)^k \tag{22}$$

$$= \left(\frac{b}{b+1}\right)^a\left(I - \frac{M}{b+1}\right)^{-a}, \tag{23}$$

the convergence of the infinite matrix series being assured by virtue of the fact that all the eigenvalues of $M/(b+1)$ are less than one in absolute value.**

*The name "negative binomial" arises from use of the following identity for binomial coefficients in (21):

$$\binom{a+k-1}{k} = (-1)^k\binom{-a}{k}.$$

See Feller [10, p.165].

**When x is a scalar, we know the binomial expansion

$$\sum_{k=0}^\infty \binom{-a}{k}(-1)^k x^k = (1-x)^{-a}$$

is valid provided $|x| < 1$. The corresponding matrix expansion

$$\sum_{k=0}^\infty \binom{-a}{k}(-1)^k A^k = (I-A)^{-a}$$

is valid provided all the eigenvalues of the square matrix A are less than one in absolute value. See Gantmacher [11, p.113]. In (22), $A = M/(b+1)$ and M, being a transition probability matrix, has 1 as its largest eigenvalue. Since $b > 0$, the eigenvalues of A are indeed all less than one in absolute value and the step from (22) to (23) is valid.

We refer to Spilerman [45] for further development of this extension of the Stayer-Mover model. He shows how to estimate the parameters a and b as well as the matrix M from empirical data on observed transitions in the population of workers, discusses testing the model, works through an example using simulated data, mentions the use of the "spiked gamma" (reserving a positive probability for Stayers, corresponding to $\lambda = 0$), and finally applies the model to real data on residential mobility in the United States.

The foregoing extension, like the Stayer-Mover model, modified the homogeneity assumption of the basic Markov chain model. Heterogeneity of the population was expressed by variations in the rate of mobility among workers. But all workers follow the same transition probability matrix and the transition rate λ for each individual is fixed over the entire period of observation. Critiques of this assumption and other ways of handling the temporal variation in the parameter λ are discussed by Ginsberg [15], Mayer [28], and Sorensen [44]. The assumption of a single transition matrix for all workers is dropped by McFarland [30] and Spilerman [46].

McFarland keeps the Markov property, the stationarity and regularity assumptions of the simple Markov chain model, but abandons population homogeneity by assuming different workers can have different transition probability matrices. He introduces a parameter m and lets $P(m)$, with entries $p_{ij}(m)$, denote a transition probability matrix of type m. (The Stayer-Mover model has $m = 2$ types of transition matrices. See Exercise 5.) How shall these matrices be combined so as to obtain a mean one-step transition matrix, say Q, for the entire population? Let $X(m)$ denote the diagonal matrix whose i-th diagonal entry $x_i(m)$ is the proportion of workers in category i at time 0 who move according to the transition probability matrix $P(m)$. Then the expected proportion of workers in category i at time 0 who end up in category j at time 1 is given by

$$q_{ij} = \sum_m x_i(m) p_{ij}(m)$$

where the sum is taken over all possible values of the parameter m. In matrix notation,

$$Q = \sum_m X(m) P(m). \tag{24}$$

Similarly, since those workers with transition probability matrix $P(m)$ have n-step transition matrix $P^n(m)$, the average or mean n-step transition matrix for the entire population is given by

$$Q^{(n)} = \sum_m X(m) P^n(m). \tag{25}$$

Because of the weighting factor $X(m)$, now $Q^{(n)}$ is *not* in general equal to the n-th power of Q. Since $P(m)$ is regular, $P^n(m) \to W(m)$ as $n \to \infty$, where $W(m)$ has identical rows, each row being the unique fixed-point probability vector associated with the matrix $P(m)$. Letting $n \to \infty$ in (25),

$$Q^{(n)} \to \sum_m X(m)W(m) = Q^*, \text{ say.}$$

Now the constant limiting population transition matrix Q^* need not, as in the basic Markov chain model, have identical rows. It follows that the long-run proportion of workers in a given state will, in general, depend on the initial state distribution.

The averaging represented by (24) has an important consequence which relates it to the so-called Cornell Mobility Model (see McGinnis [31], Henry, McGinnis, and Tegtmeyer [17]). In this model an assumption of "cumulative inertia" or "duration of stay" is made: the longer in one's current work category, the higher the probability of staying there for yet another time period. Thus the transition probability of going from state i to state j in n periods of time depends not only on i, j, and n (as in Markov models) but also on how long the worker has been in state i. The process is now non-Markovian, a fact that creates analytic difficulties. Comments on the cumulative inertia hypothesis, tests of its applicability, and extensions can be found in Hodge [18], Land [24], Morrison [32], Myers, McGinnis, and Masnick [33], Schinnar and Stewman [40], and Tuma [49]. Ginsberg [14] has reformulated McGinnis' assumptions so changes of state occur according to a Markov chain, but the time intervals between changes are random variables. Such a stochastic process is known as a semi-Markov or Markov renewal process. He also discusses the relation of this more analytically sophisticated mobility model to the Stayer-Mover model of BKM. Gilbert [13] extended Ginsberg's model to include open system mobility processes, i.e., ones allowing migration of new workers into the system. For a treatment of semi-Markov and related stochastic processes, see the paper by Pyke [37] or the appropriate sections of the books by Hoel, Port, and Stone [19], Karlin [21], or Ross [38]. The general issue of compatibility of observed data with a finite-state continuous time Markov process is treated by Singer and Spilerman [42].

The averaging in (24) of workers with different transition probability matrices also leads to observed declines in mobility rates over time, although the probabilities of movement do not themselves change for any worker. For, in McFarland's own words [30, p.470]:

> Now those who leave the given status during the first time interval differ from those who remain, in that the latter tend to be persons with higher probabilities of staying than the former. Thus the group remaining after one time period will have a higher average probability of staying than did the original group; and hence the expected proportion of the former group remaining throughout the second time period is larger than the expected proportion of the initial group remaining throughout the first time period.

Thus this model gives rise to empirical consequences which appear, at first glance, as if the probability of movement declines over time. But in fact the probabilities do not decline; it is just that those with high probabilities of movement tend to move early, and those still remaining after several time periods are predominantly persons with low probabilities of movement.

We close this review by citing some additional references for further reading. Konda and Stewman [23] and Stewman [47] describe a number of Markovian models and also a vacancy chain model due to White [50] for individual mobility in an organization. Sandefur [39] uses a nonstationary Markov model to study job changes within and across organizations. An extensive analysis and evaluation of the state of Markov model building for intragenerational occupational mobility has been contributed by Stewman [48].

All of these models make the questionable assumption that individuals behave independently of each other, that interaction among individuals is absent. It would be more realistic to suppose that the transition probabilities governing an individual's moves among occupational or social states depend on how all other individuals in the population are distributed among the states. Such so-called *interactive* Markov chain models were introduced by Conlisk [8] and further studied by Brumelle and Gerchak [5] and Lehoczky [25]. They are likely to see increased use as the theory is developed.

Finally, there are five books that deserve mention. McCall [29] makes significant use of the Stayer-Mover model in an attempt to understand income mobility with special emphasis on poverty dynamics. Pullum [36] concentrates on quantitative techniques for detecting patterns or regularities in a mobility table. A chapter in Fararo [9] and an entire volume by Boudon [4] survey the mathematical and statistical literature on mobility. Bartholomew [1] concentrates on stochastic models and includes social and occupational mobility among social phenomena to which the mathematical theory is applied.

Exercises

1. Prove the final part (c) of Result 3 which asserts that as $n \to \infty$ the state probability vector $\mathbf{f}^{(n)}$ approaches the fixed-point probability vector $\mathbf{w}$ of the transition probability matrix P. In particular, note how the initial state probability vector $\mathbf{f}^{(0)}$, present in formula (5) for $\mathbf{f}^{(n)}$, disappears in the limit.

2. This example of the Stayer-Mover model is taken from BKM [3, p.325]. Consider only three states of employment numbered 1, 2, 3 (three industries, say) with each worker occupying one of these states at each

time period (quarter year). At the start, 20% of all workers are in industry 1, 50% in industry 2, and 30% in industry 3. Suppose the proportion of Stayers in each industry is given by $s_1 = 0.40$, $s_2 = 0.50$, $s_3 = 0.30$ and that Movers follow the transition probability matrix

$$M = \begin{pmatrix} 0.90 & 0.05 & 0.05 \\ 0.10 & 0.80 & 0.10 \\ 0.20 & 0.20 & 0.60 \end{pmatrix}.$$

(a) Show that the fixed-point probability vector of M is

$$\mathbf{w} = (4/7 \ \ 2/7 \ \ 1/7).$$

(b) Show that

$$\lim_{n \to \infty} P^{(n)} = \begin{pmatrix} 26/35 & 6/35 & 3/35 \\ 4/14 & 9/14 & 1/14 \\ 2/5 & 1/5 & 2/5 \end{pmatrix}.$$

(c) Compute $\lim_{n \to \infty} \mathbf{f}^{(n)}$ and show that in the long run about 41% of all workers end up in industry 1, 42% in industry 2, and 17% in industry 3.

(d) Show that 31% of the workers in industry 1 after one quarter are Stayers and that 20% is the fraction of Stayers in industry 1 in the long run.

3. In the basic Markov chain model, the transition probability p_{ij} is the conditional probability of *arriving at* state j on the *next* trial, given that the worker is in state i now. Let $\tilde{p}_{ij}$ denote the conditional probability of *coming from* state j on the *preceding* trial, given that the worker is in state i now.

(a) Show that $\tilde{p}_{ij} = p_{ji} \dfrac{f_j^{(n)}}{f_i^{(n+1)}}$ for $n = 1, 2, \ldots$.

(b) Suppose the Markov chain is regular with fixed-point probability vector $\mathbf{w}$. Show that in the limit as $n \to \infty$,

$$\tilde{p}_{ij} = p_{ji} \frac{w_j}{w_i}.$$

(c) A Markov chain is said to be *reversible* if $P = (p_{ij})$ is equal to $\tilde{P} = (\tilde{p}_{ij})$, with $\tilde{p}_{ij}$ as in (b). Interpret such a probability process in terms of steady-state worker mobility among occupational states. (See Kemeny and Snell [22].)

4. With $r_k(t)$ defined by (19) and f the gamma density in (20), derive the negative binomial distribution given in (21) for the number of transitions made by a randomly selected worker. (*Hint*. From the definition of the gamma function, integration by parts shows that $\Gamma(a) = (a-1)\Gamma(a-1)$. Repeated application starting with $\Gamma(a+k)$ yields the formula

$$\frac{\Gamma(a+k)}{\Gamma(a)} = (a+k-1)(a+k-2)\ldots(a+1)(a),$$

needed in the derivation.)

5. With notation as in the paragraph leading to equation (24), suppose there are $m = 2$ different transition probability matrices: $P(1) = I$, the identity matrix, and $P(2) = M$, an arbitrary transition matrix. Suppose $x_i(1) = s_i$ is the proportion of workers in occupational category (state) i at time 0 who follow $P(1)$. Show in this special case that the mean one-step transition matrix Q given by (24) reduces to the corresponding matrix (12) for the Stayer-Mover model.

6. Let $P(a) = \begin{pmatrix} a & 1-a \\ 1-a & a \end{pmatrix}$. Consider the following transition probability matrices governing trial-by-trial movements between two states: (*i*) $P(1)$, (*ii*) $P(1/2)$, (*iii*) $P(0)$. In (*i*), there is complete immobility since the state is certain not to change from one trial to the next. Prais [34,35] defines a system with P in the form (*ii*) as showing perfect mobility. Here the final state is independent of the initial state since P has identical rows. The matrix in (*iii*) also represents an extreme of movement since the state is sure to change from one trial to the next.

(a) Evaluate the determinant of each of the matrices in (*i*)–(*iii*) and note that $\det(P)$ can be taken as a simple measure of mobility in the 2-state case.

(b) Would $\det(P)$ be a satisfactory measure for mobility for a transition probability matrix P with more than two states?

7. Bartholomew [1, p.24] has suggested

$$D = \sum_{i=1}^{N} \sum_{j=1}^{N} w_i |j - i| p_{ij}$$

as a measure of mobility. D is the overall mean distance traveled in one trial in the long run (i.e., at equilibrium), where "distance" is the numerical difference between the beginning and the final state. Define $D = 0$ if $p_{ii} = 1$ for all i.

(a) If $N = 2$ and P is not the identity matrix, show that

$$D = \frac{2p_{12}p_{21}}{p_{12} + p_{21}}.$$

(b) Evaluate D for the transition probability matrices defined in (i)–(iii) of the preceding exercise. Does D appear to be a satisfactory measure of mobility in the two-state case?

(c) Verify [1, p.25] that $D = 9/14$ if

$$P = \begin{pmatrix} 0.4 & 0.3 & 0.3 \\ 0.2 & 0.5 & 0.3 \\ 0.2 & 0.2 & 0.6 \end{pmatrix}.$$

8. In the basic N-state Markov chain model, suppose a worker is initially in state k and let X denote the duration of stay, i.e., the number of trials the worker is in state k before moving to another state. Assume no diagonal element of the transition probability matrix P is equal to 1.

   (a) Show that the discrete random variable X has a geometric distribution.

   (b) Show that $E(X) = 1/(1 - p_{kk})$.

   (c) Prais [34] suggests using the set of numbers

$$\mu_k^* = \frac{1 - w_k}{1 - p_{kk}} \quad (k = 1, 2, \ldots, N)$$

   where w_k is the equilibrium long-run probability that the worker is in state k, as a measure of mobility. Show that $w_k = p_{kk}$ and hence $\mu_k^* = 1$ for the perfectly mobile system characterized by a matrix P with identical rows.

9. Suppose transitions between two occupational states occur monthly, but observations of the worker population can be made only quarterly. The probability matrix

$$P = \begin{pmatrix} 1/3 & 2/3 \\ 2/3 & 1/3 \end{pmatrix}$$

   is found to govern transitions from one quarter to the next. Show that the matrix

$$Q = \tfrac{1}{2} \begin{pmatrix} 1 - 1/\sqrt[3]{3} & 1 + 1/\sqrt[3]{3} \\ 1 + 1/\sqrt[3]{3} & 1 - 1/\sqrt[3]{3} \end{pmatrix}$$

   is the unique probability matrix which is the cube root of P, i.e., Q is the unique solution of the matrix equation $P = Q^3$. (Thus the quarterly process governed by P can be *embedded* in the Markov chain with the month-by-month transition probability matrix Q. This numerical example is used by Singer and Spilerman [41, p.361] to illustrate the general embeddability problem for Markov models.)

10. Suppose transitions among three occupational states occur quarterly, but observations of the worker population are made only each six months. The probability matrix

$$I = \begin{pmatrix} 1 & 0 & 0 \\ 0 & 1 & 0 \\ 0 & 0 & 1 \end{pmatrix}$$

is found to govern transitions from one six-month period to the next. Thus, when viewed each six months, this appears to be a perfectly immobile population. Show, however, that the identity matrix I has the following four distinct square roots:

$$I, \quad A = \begin{pmatrix} 0 & 0 & 1 \\ 0 & 1 & 0 \\ 1 & 0 & 0 \end{pmatrix}, \quad B = \begin{pmatrix} 0 & 1 & 0 \\ 1 & 0 & 0 \\ 0 & 0 & 1 \end{pmatrix}, \quad C = \begin{pmatrix} 1 & 0 & 0 \\ 0 & 0 & 1 \\ 0 & 1 & 0 \end{pmatrix},$$

each of which can describe the quarter-by-quarter transitions of an underlying Markov chain mobility model. Thus conclude that if special observations over a single quarterly period can be arranged, then the particular underlying Markov quarter-by-quarter transition probability matrix can be identified. But there is no way to discriminate among I, A, B, C as the underlying transition matrix if further observations are made at six-month intervals. (This example is taken from Singer and Spilerman [41, pp.361–363] who conclude that "it is often desirable to take observations at time points which are not evenly spaced if you want to discriminate between substantively distinct stochastic models all compatible with data from a few periods.")

Bibliography

1. Bartholomew, D. J., *Stochastic Models for Social Processes*, second edition, New York: Wiley-Interscience, 1974; third edition, 1982.
2. Bhat, U. N., *Elements of Applied Stochastic Processes*, New York: Wiley, 1972.
3. Blumen, I., M. Kogan, and P. J. McCarthy, *The Industrial Mobility of Labor as a Probability Process*, Ithaca: Cornell University Press, 1955. A selection from this book is reprinted under the title "Probability Models for Mobility," pp.318–334 in Lazersfeld, P. F. and N. W. Henry (Eds.), *Readings in Mathematical Social Science*, Cambridge: M.I.T. Press, 1966.
4. Boudon, R., *Mathematical Structures of Social Mobility*, San Francisco: Jossey-Bass, 1973.
5. Brumelle, S. L. and Y. Gerchak, "A Stochastic Model Allowing Interaction Among Individuals and Its Behavior for Large Populations," *Journal of Mathematical Sociology*, vol. 7 (1980), 73–90.
6. Chung, K. L., *Markov Chains with Stationary Transition Probabilities*, second edition, New York: Springer-Verlag, 1967.
7. Chung, K. L., *Elementary Probability Theory with Stochastic Processes*, New York: Springer-Verlag, 1979.

8. Conlisk, J., "Interactive Markov Chains," *Journal of Mathematical Sociology*, vol. 4 (1976), 157–185.
9. Fararo, T. J., *Mathematical Sociology*, New York: Wiley, 1973.
10. Feller, W., *An Introduction to Probability Theory and its Applications*, vol. 1, third edition, New York: Wiley, 1968.
11. Gantmacher, F. R., *The Theory of Matrices*, New York: Chelsea, 1959.
12. Gaver, D. P. and G. L. Thompson, *Programming and Probability Models in Operations Research*, Monterey: Brooks-Cole, 1973.
13. Gilbert, G., "Semi-Markov Processes and Mobility: A Note," *Journal of Mathematical Sociology*, vol. 3 (1973), 139–145.
14. Ginsberg, R. B., "Semi-Markov Processes and Mobility," *Journal of Mathematical Sociology*, vol. 1 (1971), 233–262.
15. Ginsberg, R. B., "Stochastic Models of Residential and Geographic Mobility for Heterogeneous Populations," *Environment and Planning*, vol. 5 (1973), 113–124.
16. Goodman, L. A., "Statistical Methods for the 'Mover-Stayer' Model," *Journal of the American Statistical Association*, vol. 56 (1961), 841–868.
17. Henry, N. W., R. McGinnis, and H. W. Tegtmeyer, "A Finite Model of Mobility," *Journal of Mathematical Sociology*, vol. 1 (1971), 107–118.
18. Hodge, R. W., "Occupational Mobility as a Probability Process," *Demography*, vol. 3 (1966), 19–34.
19. Hoel, P., S. C. Port, and C. J. Stone, *Introduction to Stochastic Processes*, Boston: Houghton Mifflin, 1972.
20. Isaacson, D. L. and R. W. Madsen, *Markov Chains: Theory and Applications*, New York: Wiley, 1976.
21. Karlin, S., *A First Course in Stochastic Processes*, second edition, New York: Academic Press, 1975.
22. Kemeny, J. G. and J. L. Snell, *Finite Markov Chains*, New York: Springer-Verlag, 1976.
23. Konda, S. L. and S. Stewman, "An Opportunity Labor Demand Model and Markovian Labor Supply Models: Comparative Tests in an Organization," *American Sociological Review*, vol. 45 (1980), 276–301.
24. Land, K. D., "Duration of Residence and Prospective Migration: Further Evidence," *Demography*, vol. 6 (1969), 133–140.
25. Lehoczky, J. D., "Approximations for Interactive Markov Chains in Discrete and Continuous Time," *Journal of Mathematical Sociology*, vol. 7 (1980), 139–157.
26. Mahoney, T. A. and G. T. Milkovich, "The Internal Labor Market as a Stochastic Process," in Bartholomew, D. J. and A. R. Smith (Eds.), *Manpower and Management Science*, Lexington, Mass.: Heath, 1971.
27. Maki, D. P. and M. Thompson, *Mathematical Models and Applications*, Englewood Cliffs: Prentice-Hall, 1973.
28. Mayer, T. F., "Models of Intra-generational Mobility," pp.308–357 in Berger, J., M. Zelditch, and B. Anderson (Eds.), *Sociological Theories in Progress*, New York: Houghton Mifflin, 1972.
29. McCall, J. J., *Income Mobility, Racial Discrimination, and Economic Growth*, Lexington, Mass.: Heath, 1973.
30. McFarland, D., "Intragenerational Social Mobility as a Markov Process: Including a Time-Stationary Markovian Model that Explains Observed

Declines in Mobility Rates over Time," *American Sociological Review*, vol. 35 (1970), 463–476.

31. McGinnis, R., "A Stochastic Model of Social Mobility," *American Sociological Review*, vol. 33 (1968), 712–721.

32. Morrison, P. A., "Duration of Residence and Prospective Migration: The Evaluation of a Stochastic Model," *Demography*, vol. 4 (1967), 554–561.

33. Myers, G. C., R. McGinnis, and G. Masnick, "The Duration of Residence Approach to a Dynamic Stochastic Model of Internal Migration: A Test of the Axiom of Cumulative Inertia," *Eugenics Quarterly*, vol. 14 (1967), 121–126.

34. Prais, S. J., "Measuring Social Mobility," *Journal of the Royal Statistical Society*, Series A, vol. 118 (1955), 56–66.

35. Prais, S. J., "The Formal Theory of Social Mobility," *Population Studies*, vol. 9 (1955), 72–81.

36. Pullum, T., *Measuring Occupational Mobility*, New York: Elsevier, 1975.

37. Pyke, R., "Markov Renewal Processes: Definitions and Preliminary Properties," *Annals of Mathematical Statistics*, vol. 32 (1961), 1231–1242.

38. Ross, S. M., *Applied Probability Models with Optimization Applications*, San Francisco: Holden-Day, 1970.

39. Sandefur, G. D., "Organizational Boundaries and Upward Job Shifts," *Social Science Research*, vol. 10 (1981), 67–82.

40. Schinnar, A. P. and S. Stewman, "A Class of Markov Models of Social Mobility with Duration Memory Patterns," *Journal of Mathematical Sociology*, vol. 6 (1978), 61–86.

41. Singer, B. and S. Spilerman, "Social Mobility Models for Heterogeneous Populations," pp.356–401 in Costner, H. L. (Ed.), *Sociological Methodology 1973-1974*, San Francisco: Jossey-Bass, 1974.

42. Singer, B. and S. Spilerman, "The Representation of Social Processes by Markov Models," *American Journal of Sociology*, vol. 82 (1976), 1–54.

43. Snell, J. L., *Introduction to Probability Theory with Computing*, Englewood Cliffs: Prentice-Hall, 1975.

44. Sorensen, A. B., "The Structure of Intragenerational Mobility," *American Sociological Review*, vol. 40 (1975), 456–471.

45. Spilerman, S., "Extensions of the Mover-Stayer Model," *American Journal of Sociology*, vol. 78 (1972), 599–626.

46. Spilerman, S., "The Analysis of Mobility Processes by the Introduction of Independent Variables into a Markov Chain," *American Sociological Review*, vol. 37 (1972), 277–294.

47. Stewman, S., "Two Markov Models of Open System Occupational Mobility: Underlying Conceptualizations and Empirical Tests," *American Sociological Review*, vol. 40 (1975), 298–321.

48. Stewman, S., "Markov Models of Occupational Mobility: Theoretical Development and Empirical Support. Part 1: Careers, Part 2: Continuously Operative Job Systems," *Journal of Mathematical Sociology*, vol. 4 (1976), 201–245, 247–278.

49. Tuma, N. B., "Rewards, Resources, and the Rate of Mobility: A Nonstationary Multivariate Stochastic Model," *American Sociological Review*, vol. 41 (1976), 338–360.

50. White, H., *Chains of Opportunity: System Models of Mobility in Organizations*, Cambridge, Mass.: Harvard University Press, 1970.

Chapter 7
Recall From Memory

1. Introduction

Much information, learned over the years by each of us and somehow stored in our brains, can be brought forward and made available when required. The way in which items are recalled from long-term memory was the subject of a series of experiments conducted by Bousfield and Sedgewick [3]. These authors asked subjects to name, as quickly as possible, as many cities in the U. S. as they can. For each subject, every name was recorded along with the time it was announced. Not surprisingly, responses occur at first rapidly and with relative ease. After a time, recall becomes slower and more difficult and the subject appears to be making an effort to bring forth new responses.

The data reported by these authors and others who have studied free recall (for example, Indow and Togano [8], Johnson, Johnson, and Mark [9], Kaplan and Carvellas [10], Patterson, Meltzer, and Mandler [16]) are consistent with the following hypotheses: (i) a subject has a finite number, say c, of relevant responses stored in memory and (ii) the rate at which responses are emitted is proportional to the number of relevant items in memory but not yet recalled. If $n(t)$ denotes the number of items recalled by time t, these hypotheses are embodied in the differential equation

$$\frac{dn}{dt} = k(c - n) \tag{1}$$

where $k > 0$ is the constant of proportionality. With the initial condition $n(0) = 0$, the solution of this differential equation is seen to be

$$n(t) = c(1 - e^{-kt}). \tag{2}$$

Two examples of experimental data illustrating this exponentially damped accumulation of recalled items are shown in Figure 1. Circles and crosses indicate the actual data obtained with university students in Tokyo who were asked to recall names of animals and of females, respectively. The corresponding fitted curves of the form (2) are also sketched.

Most subjects report annoyance, especially in the latter part of the experiment, by persistent occurrences of already-mentioned names that cannot be counted again. To minimize repetition of previously recalled

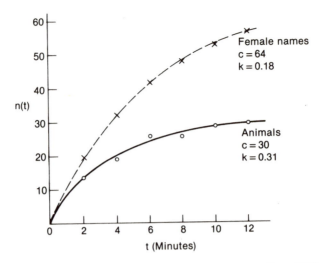

Figure 1. Two Retrieval Functions (Indow and Togano [8, p.318]).

items, suppose some constraint is placed on subjects that somehow restricts their memory search. For example, Indow and Togano report data from an experiment in which subjects were asked to list cities in Japan with the condition that they start from the furthest north and proceed toward the south. Without such a condition, the result has the exponential form seen in Figure 1. But with this restriction, the cumulative total number of items recalled becomes linearly dependent on time. (See Figure 2, where the records of two different subjects are plotted.)

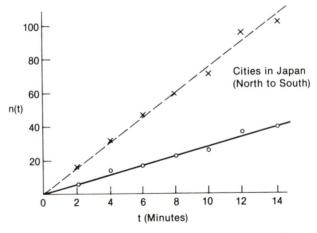

Figure 2. Two Retrieval Functions With Scanning Route Predetermined (Indow and Togano [8, p.320]).

In this unit, the exponentially damped and the linear accumulation of recalled items will be generated in two versions of a probabilistic model of memory recall suggested by J. C. Falmagne and G. Iverson.

2. The Model

We make the following assumptions governing the content of memory (Axiom 1) and the rules for recall of items from memory (Axioms 2–4).

Axiom 1. A total of c items (belonging to a particular category like U. S. cities, names of girls, etc.) have been faithfully coded and stored in memory by the subject. Each item is assumed to be equally accessible for recall.

Axiom 2. Items are randomly sampled from memory, one at a time, and with replacement (Version A) or without replacement (Version B). Thus we have two versions of this Axiom depending on whether an item, once sampled, is replaced and can be sampled again (Version A), or is not replaced and therefore cannot be sampled again (Version B).

Axiom 3. An item sampled is first examined as to its output status. It is itself output (i.e., announced as a new response of the subject) if and only if it has not previously been output.

Axiom 4. The times required for examining sampled items are independent, identically distributed random variables, each with exponential density given by

$$f(t) = \begin{cases} \lambda e^{-\lambda t} & \text{if } t \geq 0 \\ 0 & \text{if } t < 0 \end{cases} \qquad (3)$$

where $\lambda > 0$ is a positive constant. (The mean examination time, given by the integral $\int_0^\infty t f(t)\, dt$, is easily verified to equal $1/\lambda$.)

This exponential density function can be understood as arising from a limit argument common in probability theory. (See, for example, Feller [6, pp.157,458].) Imagine time divided into processing units $1, 2, \ldots$ in each of which an item recalled (an input to the processor) is examined and classified as a success (S) if new and therefore suitable for output, or as a failure (F) if unsuitable because of it having already been used. Suppose these inputs are independent and the probability of each being S is p. Let T_1 denote the time (starting at $t = 0$) until the first output is made. then

$$\Pr(T_1 \leq k) = 1 - (1-p)^k \quad (k = 1, 2, \ldots) \qquad (4)$$

since the event "$T_1 \leq k$" means that at least one of the first k items is S or, equivalently, that not all are F's.

Now refine this discrete time scale by supposing inputs occur at time $\Delta t, 2\Delta t, \ldots$. As $\Delta t \to 0$ we require that p also approach zero, but in such a way that the success rate $\frac{p}{\Delta t} = \lambda$, say, stays fixed. Now if $k \to \infty$, $\Delta t \to 0$, and $k\Delta t \to t \geq 0$, then in the limit, (4) becomes

$$\Pr(T_1 \leq t) = \lim_{\Delta t \to 0} [1 - (1 - \lambda\Delta t)^{\frac{t}{\Delta t}}]$$
$$= 1 - e^{-\lambda t},$$

which is recognized as the cumulative distribution function corresponding to the exponential density function given in (3). (For other demonstrations of this exponential as the limit of the geometric distribution, see Bush and Mosteller [4] or McGill [13].)

The following notation will be used in the analysis of Axioms 1–4 and their consequences.

$N(t)$ = number of items recalled from the initial time $t = 0$ to time t.

$P_n(t) = \Pr(N(t) = n)$ $(n = 0, 1, \ldots, c)$.

T_1 = time from 0 to the first output item.

T_i = ith interarrival time, i.e., the elapsed time between the $(i - 1)$st and the ith output item $(i = 2, 3, \ldots, c)$.

W_i = waiting time from 0 to the ith output item $(i = 1, 2, \ldots, c)$.

K_i = number of examinations required to produce the ith new item for $i = 1, 2, \ldots, c$, i.e., the number of examinations of sampled items when there are $i-1$ items already announced, up to and including the examination which finally shows a sampled item to be new and not previous output.

3.   Outline of the Analysis

Our aim is to obtain a formula for $P_n(t)$. It will be helpful to keep in mind the following steps to be followed in reaching this goal.

Step 1.   Determine $\Pr(K_i = k)$, the probability distribution of the random variable K_i.

Step 2.   Determine $\Pr(T_i \leq t \mid K_i = k)$, the conditional distribution function of the ith interarrival time given the value of K_i and thus find the (cumulative) distribution function of T_i using the equation

$$\Pr(T_i \leq t) = \sum_{k=1}^{\infty} \Pr(K_i = k)\Pr(T_i \leq t \mid K_i = k). \qquad (5)$$

Step 3.   Compute the probability density function of T_i by differentiating its distribution function (5).

Step 4.   Determine the probability density function of the random variable W_j for $j = 1, 2, \ldots, c$ by using

$$W_j = \sum_{i=1}^{j} T_i, \qquad (6)$$

an identity that follows directly from the meaning of the symbols.

Step 5. Determine $P_n(t)$ by means of the formulas

$$P_n(t) = \begin{cases} 1 - \Pr(W_1 \leq t) & \text{if } n = 0 \\ \Pr(W_n \leq t) - \Pr(W_{n+1} \leq t) & \text{if } n = 1, 2, \ldots, c. \end{cases} \quad (7)$$

The formula for $P_0(t)$ follows from the fact that the event "$N(t) = 0$" means the waiting time until the first output item exceeds t. The formula for $P_n(t)$ when $n > 0$ follows from the observation that one is left with the event "$N(t) = n$" when one deletes from the experimental outcomes for which the waiting time until the nth output item is at most t all those for which the $(n + 1)$st output item also occurs by time t. To make (7) correct when $n = c$, the value 0 is assigned to $\Pr(W_{c+1} \leq t)$.

4. The Derivation of $P_n(t)$

We turn now to the details involved in carrying out these steps in the case of Version A (sampling with replacement in Axiom 2). Results are numbered $1A$, $2A$, etc. to make their dependence on this version of Axiom 2 clear. The derivation of $P_n(t)$ in the case of Version B of Axiom 2 (sampling without replacement) is left for the Exercises.

Theorem 1A.

$$\Pr(K_1 = k) = \begin{cases} 1 & \text{if } k = 1 \\ 0 & \text{if } k = 2, 3, \ldots, \end{cases} \quad (8)$$

and for $i = 2, 3 \ldots, c$,

$$\Pr(K_i = k) = (1 - p_i)^{k-1} p_i \quad (k = 1, 2, \ldots) \quad (9)$$

where

$$p_i = \frac{c - i + 1}{c}. \quad (10)$$

Proof. If there are no items already announced, then the first sampled item is guaranteed to be the first output. Hence K_1 equals 1 with certainty as claimed in equation (8). If there are $i - 1$ different items already recalled, then a randomly sampled item from the c available items is new with probability p_i given by (10). The event $K_i = k$ means that the first $(k-1)$ sampled items are not new and the kth item is new. Since sampling is with replacement the probability p_i is the probability that *each* sampled item is new and $(1 - p_i)$ the probability that it is not new. Thus we are led to formula (9). Note that this formula, properly interpreted, actually includes formula (8) when i is put equal to 1.

If k examinations are required for the recall of the ith item, then the ith interarrival time T_i is the sum of k independent random variables, each with the exponential density given by (3). The following Lemma will prove helpful in carrying out Step 2.

Lemma 1. Let $X_1, X_2, \ldots, X_n$ be n independent and identically distributed random variables, each exponentially distributed with density function given by (3). Then $X_1 + X_2 + \cdots + X_n$ has a *gamma distribution* with parameters n and λ, i.e., the sum has density function f given by

$$f(x) = \begin{cases} \lambda e^{-\lambda x} \dfrac{(\lambda x)^{n-1}}{(n-1)!} & \text{if } x \geq 0 \\ 0 & \text{if } x < 0. \end{cases} \tag{11}$$

This Lemma appears in many standard textbooks on probability, mathematical statistics, and queueing theory. For a proof by mathematical induction see Ross [17, p.114]. A proof using moment generating functions (Exercise 1) is given by Meyer [15, p.221], and one using Laplace transforms by Kleinrock [12, p.71]. (In queueing theory, the gamma densities in (11) are referred to as the family of Erlang distributions.)

From the Lemma and Axiom 4, the formula

$$\Pr(T_i \leq t \mid K_i = k) = \int_0^t \lambda e^{-\lambda t} \frac{(\lambda t)^{k-1}}{(k-1)!} \, dt \quad (k = 1, 2, \ldots) \tag{12}$$

is immediate. Step 2 is now done and $\Pr(T_i \leq t)$ can be written using (9) and (12) in formula (5). The resulting expression for the distribution function of T_i can be simplified:

$$\begin{aligned}
\Pr(T_i \leq t) &= \sum_{k=1}^{\infty} (1 - p_i)^{k-1} p_i \int_0^t \lambda e^{-\lambda t} \frac{(\lambda t)^{k-1}}{(k-1)!} \, dt \\
&= p_i \lambda \int_0^t e^{-\lambda t} \sum_{k=1}^{\infty} \frac{[\lambda t (1 - p_i)]^{k-1}}{(k-1)!} \, dt \\
&= p_i \lambda \int_0^t e^{-\lambda t} e^{\lambda t (1 - p_i)} \, dt \\
&= p_i \lambda \int_0^t e^{-\lambda p_i t} \, dt \\
&= 1 - e^{-\lambda p_i t}.
\end{aligned}$$

Since the probability density function of T_i is obtained by differentiation, we have proved the following result.

Theorem 2A. The random variable T_i, the elapsed time between the $(i-1)$st and the ith output item, is exponentially distributed with density given by

$$f_i(t) = \begin{cases} \lambda_i e^{-\lambda_i t} & \text{if } t \geq 0 \\ 0 & \text{if } t < 0 \end{cases} \tag{13}$$

where $\lambda_i = \lambda p_i$. (Note that $\lambda_1 = \lambda$, so (13), as expected, gives the correct exponential density for T_1 and thus holds for $i = 1, 2, \ldots, c$.)

Step 4 of our previously outlined program is next. Since we know $W_j = T_1 + T_2 + \cdots + T_j$ and the random variables T_i are independent, the following Lemma will be helpful in obtaining the density function of the W's from the known density function of the T's.

Lemma 2. Let X and Y be independent random variables with density functions f and g, respectively. Suppose $f(t) = g(t) = 0$ if $t < 0$. If h is the density function of $X + Y$, then

$$h(t) = \int_0^t f(t - s)g(s)\,ds. \tag{14}$$

The integral in (14) is known as the *convolution* of the densities f and g. We omit a proof of this well-known result. See, for example, Meyer [15, p.257] or Ross [17, p.42].) A formula for the density function of W_j will be derived by use of this Lemma.

Theorem 3A. Let g_j denote the probability density function of W_j. Then, for any positive integer j,

$$g_j(t) = \lambda_j \binom{c}{j-1}(e^{-\lambda t/c})^{c-j+1}(1 - e^{-\lambda t/c})^{j-1} \tag{15}$$

if $t \geq 0$ and $g_j(t) = 0$ if $t < 0$.

Proof (by mathematical induction). If $j = 1$, then $W_1 = T_1$ and $g_1(t)$ should reduce to $f_1(t)$ as given by (13). This is what (15) reduces to if $j = 1$, so the induction is underway.

Now suppose (15) is true for $j = k$ and let us prove it is true for $j = k + 1$. Since $W_{k+1} = W_k + T_{k+1}$, Lemma 2 yields

$$g_{k+1}(t) = \int_0^t \lambda_{k+1} e^{-\lambda_{k+1}(t-s)} g_k(s)\,ds.$$

The induction hypothesis permits replacing $g_k(s)$ by its expression from (15). Noting that $\lambda_{k+1} = \lambda(c-k)/c$, simplifying, and making the substitution $u = e^{-\lambda s/c}$ in the integral, we find

$$g_{k+1}(t) = \lambda_{k+1} e^{-\lambda t(c-k)/c} \lambda_k \binom{c}{k-1} \int_0^t u(1-u)^{k-1}\,ds.$$

But $u\,ds = (-c/\lambda)\,du$, so the integral is easy to evaluate. Simplifying and using $\lambda_k = \lambda(c - k + 1)/c$, we obtain

$$g_{k+1}(t) = \lambda_{k+1} \frac{c-k+1}{k} \binom{c}{k-1}(e^{-\lambda t/c})^{c-k}(1 - e^{-\lambda t/c})^k.$$

Since

$$\frac{c-k+1}{k}\binom{c}{k-1}=\binom{c}{k},$$

equation (15) is verified when $j = k + 1$ and the proof by induction is complete This also completes step 4 of our program.

To find $P_n(t)$, note first that differentiating (7) yields

$$\frac{dP_n(t)}{dt} = \begin{cases} -g_1(t) & \text{if } n = 0 \\ g_n(t) - g_{n+1}(t) & \text{if } n = 1, 2, \ldots, c. \end{cases} \tag{16}$$

Lemma 3. $g_n(t) - g_{n+1}(t) = \dfrac{1}{\lambda_{n+1}}\dfrac{d}{dt}[g_{n+1}(t)] \quad n = 1, 2, \ldots, c. \tag{17}$

Proof. The simplest and most direct, but also the most tedious proof uses (15) to write each term in equation (17). Algebraic simplification then shows that the left and right sides of the equation are indeed equal. We leave this for the reader and instead outline a more advanced, indirect, but computationally simpler proof using moment generating functions.

Let $M_n(s)$ denote the m.g.f. of W_n. Since $W_n = T_1 + \cdots + T_n$ and the T's are independent random variables, M_n is the product of the m.g.f.'s of $T_1, \ldots, T_n$. But T_i is exponentially distributed with parameter λ_i (Theorem 2A) so the m.g.f. of T_i is $\lambda_i/(\lambda_i - s)$. Hence

$$M_n(s) = \frac{\lambda_1}{\lambda_1 - s} \cdot \frac{\lambda_2}{\lambda_2 - s} \cdot \ldots \cdot \frac{\lambda_n}{\lambda_n - s},$$

and

$$\frac{M_n(s)}{M_{n+1}(s)} = 1 - \frac{s}{\lambda_{n+1}}.$$

Rearranging,

$$M_n(s) - M_{n+1}(s) = \frac{1}{\lambda_{n+1}}[-sM_{n+1}(s)].$$

In integral form, this means

$$\int_0^\infty e^{st}[g_n(t) - g_{n+1}(t)]\,dt = \frac{1}{\lambda_{n+1}}(-s)\int_0^\infty e^{st}g_{n+1}(t)\,dt$$

$$= \frac{1}{\lambda_{n+1}}\int_0^\infty e^{st}\frac{d}{dt}[g_{n+1}(t)]\,dt,$$

the last equality following after integrating by parts and noting that $g_{n+1}(0) = 0$. Since

$$\int_0^\infty e^{st}u(t)\,dt = \int_0^\infty e^{st}v(t)\,dt$$

for continuous functions u and v implies $u = v$ (the uniqueness property of the Laplace transform), the proof of identity (17) of the Lemma is complete. (Additional insight into this Lemma is given by McGill and Gibbon [14,. pp.7–9], who relate it to a stochastic process and what they call the general-gamma distribution.)

Using Lemma 3 and (16), it follows immediately that

$$\frac{dP_n(t)}{dt} = \begin{cases} -g_1(t) & \text{if } n = 0 \\ \dfrac{1}{\lambda_{n+1}} \dfrac{d}{dt}[g_{n+1}(t)] & \text{if } n = 1, 2, \ldots, c. \end{cases} \tag{18}$$

Since all the densities $g_j(t)$ in (18) are known from Theorem 3A, the derivative of $P_n(t)$ is known and hence $P_n(t)$ itself can be determined. Thus

$$\frac{dP_0(t)}{dt} = -\lambda e^{-\lambda t} \tag{19}$$

and for $n = 1, 2, \ldots, c$,

$$P_n(t) = \frac{1}{\lambda_{n+1}} g_{n+1}(t) + C \tag{20}$$

where C is a constant of integration. From the meaning of $P_n(t)$ it is clear that

$$P_n(0) = \begin{cases} 1 & \text{if } n = 0 \\ 0 & \text{if } n \sim 0. \end{cases}$$

Hence by integrating (19),

$$P_0(t) = e^{-\lambda t}.$$

Since $g_{n+1}(0) = 0$ from (15), the constant C in (20) must be zero and for $n = 1, 2, \ldots, c$, we have

$$P_n(t) = \binom{c}{n}(1 - e^{-\lambda t/c})^n (e^{-\lambda t/c})^{c-n}. \tag{21}$$

(Note that this formula is also correct when $n = 0$.) We have thus proved the following result, to which all our efforts were directed.

Theorem 4A. $P_n(t)$, the probability that $N(t) = n$, is given by formula (21). In words: *the number of items recalled by time t is binomially distributed* with parameters c (corresponding to the number of Bernoulli trials) and $1 - e^{-\lambda t/c}$ (corresponding to the probability of "success" on each trial).

Since the mean of a binomially distributed random variable with parameters n and p is np, if follows that

$$E[N(t)] = c(1 - e^{-\lambda t/c}), \tag{22}$$

precisely the exponentially damped accumulation of recalled items corresponding to equation (2) and graphed in Figure 1. In the deterministic differential equation model leading to (2), the *number* of recalled items follows the exponential form. But in the stochastic model, this number becomes a random variable and it is the *mean number* of recalled items that has the corresponding exponential form specified in (22).

Dispersion about the mean is measured by the variance, which is equal to $np(1 - p)$ for a binomial random variable. In this case,

$$\text{Var}[N(t)] = c(1 - e^{-\lambda t/c})e^{-\lambda t/c}.$$

It turns out that typical values of λ/c, obtained from experimental data, are .4 or less. Therefore the variance of $N(t)$ will be small compared to the mean, even for moderate values of t. These data (Indow and Togano [8, p.320]) also support the predicted relation $k = \lambda/c$, obtained by comparing (2) and (22).

In Exercises 2–4, a proof is outlined of the following counterpart of Theorem 4A, but assuming Version B, when the random sampling of Axiom 2 is carried out *without* replacement.

Theorem 4B. $P_n(t)$, the probability that $N(t) = n$, is given by

$$P_n(t) = \frac{(\lambda t)^n}{n!}e^{-\lambda t} \quad \text{for } n = 0, 1, \ldots, c - 1 \tag{23}$$

and

$$P_c(t) = \int_0^t \lambda e^{-\lambda x}\frac{(\lambda x)^{c-1}}{(c - 1)!}\,dx. \tag{24}$$

In words: *the number of items recalled by time t follows a Poisson distribution truncated at c.*

Were the Poisson distribution not truncated, the mean and variance of $N(t)$ would each be equal to λt. Therefore, from this stochastic model, we should expect an approximate linear dependence of the mean number of words recalled by time t on the elapsed time t, as seen in Figure 2. Both the large variance and the effects of truncation should produce a good deal of variation about this straight line.

Thus the addition of a constraining condition (for example, "name all the cities you can, *but proceed from north to south*"), when subjects are instructed at the outset of the experiment, is made to correspond in the probability model to a change from sampling with replacement from memory (Axiom 2A) to sampling without replacement (Axiom 2B). As we have seen, this makes the mean number of recalled items change from an exponentially decaying growth to an approximately linear growth over time.

5. Final Remarks and Additional References

Needless to say, although the stochastic model is of mathematical interest and does capture a few of the gross features of some recall experiments, it does not supply the kind of understanding of memory sought by psychologists. Complications arising even in the sort of recall experiment outlined here are discussed by Shiffrin [19,20]. Experimental data are fitted to a hyperbolic function of the form

$$n(t) = ct/(k+t)$$

instead of the exponential in equation (2) by Gruenewald and Lockhead [7]. The notion of independence vs. dependence of memory trace storage is examined by Rotondo [18]. A summary of what he calls "sample-and-recognize models" as well as other models of retrieval from long-term memory is supplied by Baddeley [2, pp.288–299].

Atkinson and Juola [1] and Kintsch [11] treat various aspects of long-term memory, especially storage, retrieval, and search processes. Research on memory scanning is reviewed by Sternberg [21] who also discusses the use of reaction time methods to explore the processes involved in the retrieval of information from categories that are well-learned and presumably stored in long-term memory. (For short-term memory, see Deutsch and Deutsch [5].)

Finally, there is a recent article by Wickelgren [22] which reviews the literature on memory coding, processing, storage, and retrieval.

Exercises

1. Let $X_1, X_2, \ldots, X_n$ be independent, identically distributed random variables, each exponentially distributed with parameter λ. The probability density function of X_i is given in (3). Let

$$S_n = \sum_{i=1}^{n} X_i$$

(a) Show that the moment generating function (m.g.f.) of X_i is given (for $s < \lambda$) by
$$E(e^{sX_i}) = \lambda/(\lambda - s)$$
and conclude that the m.g.f. of S_n is $[\lambda/(\lambda - s)]^n$.

(b) Show that the m.g.f. of the gamma distribution with parameters n and λ, with density function given in (11), is also $[\lambda/(\lambda - s)]^n$. Thus complete the proof of Lemma 1.

Note. For the following exercises, assume Version B of Axiom 2.

2. Prove: **Theorem** 2B. The random variable T_i, the elapsed time between the $(i-1)$st and the ith output item, is exponentially distributed with probability density given by (3). *Hint.* A number of steps needed in the proof of Theorem 2A can now be bypassed and Theorem 2B can be proved directly from the Axioms.

3. Prove: **Theorem** 3B. The random variable W_n is gamma distributed with probability density given by (11). *Note.* This is the counterpart of Theorem 3A.

4. Use the formulas in (7) relating $P_n(t)$ and the cumulative distribution function of W_n to determine $P_0(t)$, $P_n(t)$ for $n = 1, 2, \ldots, c-1$, and finally $P_c(t)$. Thus verify (23) and (24), completing the proof of Theorem 4B. *Hint.* $\Pr(W_{c+1} \le t) = 0$ since it is impossible to recall more than the c responses stored in memory.

Bibliography

1. Atkinson, R. C. and J. F. Juola, "Search and Decision Processes in Recognition Memory," in Krantz, D. H., R. C. Atkinson, R. D. Luce, and P. Suppes (Eds.), *Contemporary Developments in Mathematical Psychology*, vol. 1, San Francisco: Freeman, 1974.

2. Baddeley, A. D., *The Psychology of Memory*, New York: Basic Books, 1976.

3. Bousfield, W. A. and C. H. W. Sedgewick, "An Analysis of Sequences of Restricted Associative Responses," *Journal of General Psychology*, vol. 30 (1944), 149–165.

4. Bush, R. R. and F. Mosteller, *Stochastic Models for Learning*, New York: Wiley, 1955.

5. Deutsch, D. and J. A. Deutsch (Eds.), *Short-Term Memory*, New York: Academic Press, 1975.

6. Feller, W., *An Introduction to Probability Theory and Its Applications*, vol. 1, third edition, New York: Wiley, 1968.

7. Gruenewald, P. J. and G. R. Lockhead, "The Free Recall of Category Examples," *Journal of Experimental Psychology: Human Learning and Memory*, vol. 6 (1980), 225–240.

8. Indow, T. and K. Togano, "On Retrieving Sequence from Long-Term Memory," *Psychological Review*, vol. 77 (1970), 317–331.

9. Johnson, D. M., R. C. Johnson, and A. L. Mark, "A Mathematical Analysis of Verbal Fluency," *Journal of General Psychology*, vol. 44 (1951), 121–128.

10. Kaplan, I. T. and T. Carvellas, "Response Probabilities in Verbal Recall," *Journal of Verbal Learning and Verbal Behavior*, vol. 8 (1969), 344–349.

11. Kintsch, W., *Learning, Memory, and Conceptual Processes*, New York: Wiley, 1970.

12. Kleinrock, L., *Queueing Systems*, vol. 1, New York: Wiley, 1975.

13. McGill, W. J., "Stochastic Latency Mechanisms," Chapter 6 in Luce, R. D., R. R. Bush, and E. Galanter (Eds.), *Handbook of Mathematical Psychology*, vol. 1, New York: Wiley, 1963.

14. McGill, W. J. and J. Gibbon, "The General-Gamma Distribution and Reaction Times," *Journal of Mathematical Psychology*, vol. 2 (1965), 1–18.

15. Meyer, P. L., *Introductory Probability and Statistical Applications*, second edition, Reading, Mass.: Addison-Wesley, 1970.

16. Patterson, K. E., R. H. Meltzer, and G. Mandler, "Inter-response Times in Categorized Free Recall," *Journal of Verbal Learning and Verbal Behavior*, vol. 10 (1971), 417–426.

17. Ross, S. M., *Introduction to Probability Models*, New York: Academic Press, 1972.

18. Rotondo, J. A., "Independence of Trace Storage and Organized Recall," *Journal of Verbal Learning and Verbal Behavior*, vol. 18 (1979), 675–686.

19. Shiffrin, R. M., "Forgetting: Trace Erosion or Retrieval Failure," *Science*, vol. 168 (1970), 1601–1603.

20. Shiffrin, R. M., "Memory Search," Chapter 12 in Norman, D. A. (Ed.), *Models of Human Memory*, New York: Academic Press, 1970.

21. Sternberg, S., "Memory Scanning: New Findings and Current Controversies," *Quarterly Journal of Experimental Psychology*, vol. 27 (1975), 1–32. Reprinted in a modified version in Deutsch and Deutsch [5].

22. Wickelgren, W. A., "Human Learning and Memory," *Annual Review of Psychology*, vol. 32 (1981), 21–52.

Postscript

There are a number of thoughts that come to mind after looking back over the preceding seven chapters.

In constructing a probabilistic model of some real-world phenomenon, it is tempting to assume that certain events or random variables or successive trials of an experiment are statistically independent. The temptation arises not because this is always a realistic assumption (often it is not), but rather because it has nice mathematical consequences. With an independent trials process, for example, one associates probability p_j with outcome event E_j and then the probability of the joint occurrence of event sequences like E_i, E_j, E_k is given by the simple multiplicative rule as the product $p_i p_j p_k$. One finds this independence assumption used throughout the foregoing chapters.

But one also sees various ways of modifying this assumption. In a Markov chain model, the event E_k no longer has a fixed probability p_k since the outcome of any trial is made to depend on the outcome of the immediately preceding trial. In such a model, a conditional probability p_{jk} is associated with each pair of events E_j and E_k. Given E_j has occurred at some trial, p_{jk} is the probability that E_k occurs at the next trial. If the starting trial is numbered zero and the probability of the outcome E_i at trial zero is denoted by p_i, then an outcome sequence like E_i, E_j, E_k is now assigned probability $p_i p_{ij} p_{jk}$. Such Markov chain models were introduced in Chapter 4 (Stochastic Learning Models) and in Chapter 6 (Probability Models for Mobility).

In Chapter 6, the simple Markov chain model was seen still to be an oversimplification of reality. Various ways of introducing yet more complexity into the model (two Markov chains, one for Movers and another for Stayers; transitions among states occurring randomly in time rather than at fixed time-points; etc.) have been studied. One line of research leads to more complicated and mathematically sophisticated semi-Markov or Markov renewal processes.

These particular examples seem worth pointing out here because they illustrate a general principle in mathematical modeling. Of course, one wishes to make do with the simplest possible set of assumptions in order to make the model mathematically tractable. But real-world phenomena are rarely obliging and the results, when compared to actual data, are often disappointing. One then searches for ways to weaken the assumptions, to make the model more realistic, so it captures the essential features of the real-world phenomenon under study well enough for the purposes at hand. This method of introducing complexity in stages is very typical. What is

111

remarkable is how often useful results can be obtained from models that are still simple enough to be analyzed mathematically.

Another feature worth explicit mention is exemplified by the stochastic processes introduced in Chapter 2 (How Many People Have Ever Lived?) and in Chapter 5 (Glottochronology). Now the system no longer depends on a discrete time parameter (with observations occurring only at fixed time points), but rather on a continuous time variable. In general, one studies the conditional probability $P_{jk}(s, t)$, the probability of finding the system in state E_k at time t, given that at some previous time s the system was in state E_j. Introducing time homogeneity makes $P_{jk}(s, s+t)$ depend only on the duration t of the time interval and not on s which signifies where the interval is located on the time axis. Finally, if the initial state (say, at time $t = 0$) is given, then we write $P_k(t)$ as the absolute probability of state E_k at time t.

Review of the birth and death process for population growth in Section 2.2 and of the death process for words in Section 5.2 will show that the postulates from which these absolute probabilities are determined refer only to the behavior of the transition probabilities $P_{jk}(h)$ for small values of h. What happens in a small time interval from t to $t + h$ leads, as h approaches zero, to a system of difference-differential equations from which the unknown probabilities $P_k(t)$ (for $k = 0, 1, 2, \ldots$) are able to be determined by standard methods of analysis, often involving generating functions or transforms of one kind or another. Those who go on to study the theory of stochastic processes will see this important technique used time and again. (See, for example, the introductory treatment in Feller [4, Chapter XVII].)

One cannot help observing in our seven chapters that the *mean* of some random variable is often taken as a quantity to be studied. In Chapter 2, it is the mean number of persons alive at time t, in Chapter 3 it is the mean net present value of a project that determines whether it is funded or not, in the simple learning model of Chapter 4 it is the mean number of response errors made by a subject that leads to statistical estimates of important model parameters, in Chapter 5 it is the mean number of words remaining unchanged at time t that forms the basis for language dating, and in Chapter 7 it is the mean number of items recalled by time t that is compared with experimental data.

We have pointed out in Chapter 2 how a variable of interest in a deterministic model (say, number of persons alive at time t in the customary differential equation exponential growth model) is mirrored by the *mean* of the corresponding random variable in an associated stochastic model (say, the mean number of persons alive at time t in a birth-death stochastic model). Although the number of persons alive at time t is a random variable in the probability model, its mean value has the same exponential form as the solution of the corresponding deterministic differential equation model.

As Eigen and Winkler [3, p.23] put it:

All the direct impressions and experience we receive through our senses reflect the macrocosm. But even in this realm, we have learned that events that are random if viewed individually are subject to deterministic laws in the context of large numbers.

Another feature of the mean value in applied mathematics is its widespread use as an objective function in some decision or optimization model. One frequently seeks to minimize mean cost or to maximize mean profit, for example. And, as in Chapter 3, a funding decision can be based on a project's mean net present value. In a probability model, beginners are often tempted to replace a random variable by its mean and then to proceed with the analysis as if the random variable were this constant mean value. Unfortunately, this is *not* a valid procedure since the optimal decision is likely to depend not only on the mean but also on other features of the random variable. For example, in Problem 2 of Chapter 3, the decision on whether to fund a project depends not only on the mean completion time of the project but also on the nature of the probability distribution of the random completion time.

Finally, we point out that our focus in this work has intentionally been quite narrow. We wanted to illustrate some important ideas and techniques of *probability* theory in the context of social science applications. That these topics in probability are widely used in the various social sciences is attested to by the fact that articles in over 60 different journals appear in chapter bibliographies. But much more, in probability and also in other branches of mathematics, must be learned and be available as tools for the analysis of social science phenomena. A glance at the contents of some recent books (Bartholomew [1], Bender [2], Kim and Roush [5], Olinick [6]) will show the variety of mathematical topics that have already been found useful for mathematical modeling in the social sciences. Many (linear programming and computer simulation, for example) are relatively newly developed. The beneficial symbiotic relationship between mathematics and social science is likely to continue and grow as mathematicians become increasingly interested in tackling the difficult problems arising in the social sciences and as social scientists increasingly emphasize the importance of mathematics in the training of their students.

Bibliography

1. Bartholomew, D. J., *Mathematical Methods in Social Science*, New York, Wiley, 1981.
2. Bender, E. A., *An Introduction to Mathematical Modeling*, New York: Wiley, 1978.
3. Eigen, M. and R. Winkler, *Laws of the Game, How the Principles of Nature Govern Chance*, New York: Knopf, 1981.

4. Feller, W., *An Introduction to Probability Theory and its Applications*, vol. 1, third edition, New York: Wiley, 1968.
5. Kim, K. H. and F. W. Roush, *Mathematics for Social Scientists*, New York: Elsevier, 1980.
6. Olinick, M., *An Introduction to Mathematical Models in the Social and Life Sciences*, Reading, Mass.: Addison-Wesley, 1978.

Author and Subject Index

118